John MacDevitt

Father Hand

founder of All Hallows Catholic College for the foreign missions, the story of a great servant of God

John MacDevitt

Father Hand

founder of All Hallows Catholic College for the foreign missions, the story of a great servant of God

ISBN/EAN: 9783743657885

Printed in Europe, USA, Canada, Australia, Japan

Cover: Foto ©Lupo / pixelio.de

More available books at **www.hansebooks.com**

FATHER HAND.

FATHER HAND:

FOUNDER OF ALL HALLOWS CATHOLIC COLLEGE

FOR THE FOREIGN MISSIONS.

The Story of a Great Servant of God.

BY

REV. JOHN MacDEVITT, D.D.,

Professor of the Introduction to Scripture, Ecclesiastical History, &c.,
All Hallows College, Dublin.

DUBLIN:
M. H. GILL & SON,
50 UPPER SACKVILLE STREET.

NEW YORK:
FR. PUSTET & CO.,
52 BARCLAY STREET; AND
CINCINNATI: 204 VINE STREET.

1885.

To the Memory of Him,

Who was my Dear Brother,

The Late Bishop of Raphoe,

And, who

For many Years as a Director and Professor

In All Hallows College,

Was a Devoted Follower of its Illustrious Founder,

Father Hand,

This Biography is Affectionately Dedicated

by

THE AUTHOR.

PREFACE.

THE largest Foreign Missionary College in the Catholic world was founded some forty-two years ago, near Dublin, by FATHER HAND, a holy Irish priest. In the first fervour of his ministry he dedicated himself with ardent zeal, to what he believed to be a heavenly inspiration of sending the message of salvation to English-speaking people, particularly to the poor exiles from Erin. Hence the story of his life cannot fail to be interesting, and especially welcome to all belonging to the Old Country.

Such a biography is at once a history and an argument; for it adds a bright chapter to the annals of the Irish Church, and furnishes an answer to those who represent the Catholic Clergy of Ireland as indolent and unenlightened.

It gives emphasis to the great truth of the perennial activity of Catholicism, and marks the vitality and the resiliency of the Irish race. Thus it may help to set our people in a fairer light before foreign nations, in whose mind the not uncommon prevalence of poverty and the other grievous misfortunes of our country, have come to be associated with the notion of a certain barbarism in habits and tastes.

For these amongst many other kindred reasons, this narrative has been written, without any effort at enthusiasm or panegyric, beyond the simple assertion of fact, which, indeed, is itself the highest eulogy of one, whose greatest triumph was to have achieved much and to have been little known.

ALL HALLOWS, DUBLIN,
Feast of the Epiphany, 6th January, 1885.

CONTENTS.

CHAPTER I.
MISSION OF THE SACRED ISLE . . . . Page 1

CHAPTER II.
A SCENE OF SOFT BEAUTY AND DARK SHADOWS 15

CHAPTER III.
A MOTHER'S PICTURE AND A FIRST COMMUNION 31

CHAPTER IV.
THE YOUNG SHEPHERD IS INVITED OVER TO BETHLEHEM 40

CHAPTER V.
THE STING OF DEFEAT 60

CHAPTER VI.
A RELIGIOUS AWAKENING 75

CHAPTER VII.
AN INSPIRATION 101

CHAPTER VIII.

THE CHOSEN DIRECTORS 129

CHAPTER IX.

IN THE SOLITUDE—AT THE FEET OF PETER . 162

CHAPTER X.

THE FOUNDER OF ALL HALLOWS AND THE TRIBUNE OF THE IRISH PEOPLE . . . 197

CHAPTER XI.

"THEY THAT SOW IN TEARS SHALL REAP IN JOY" 224

CHAPTER XII.

HE DIED FULL OF LABOURS, BUT NOT FULL OF DAYS 247

CHAPTER XIII.

A PORTRAIT 263

FATHER HAND.

CHAPTER I.

MISSION OF THE SACRED ISLE.

CONTENTS.—Ireland's Divine Commission to teach—Ireland's zeal in Saving the Souls of her Own Race and Creed—Spiritual Destitution of Irish Catholics Abroad in the Early Stages of the Irish Exodus—The Falling-off from the Faith on the part of the Children of Irish Catholic Emigrants—The Sorrow with which this Melancholy fact in America is Noted—Father Hand raised up by God to keep the Old Faith active among the Irish Abroad.

> Hope of my Country ! House of God !
>   All Hallows ! Blessèd feet are those
> By which thy shadowy courts are trod,
>   Ere yet the breeze of morning blows !
> Blessed are the winds that waft them forth
>   To victory over the rough sea-foam—
> Can God forget the race at home ?
>
> AUBREY DE VERE.

CHARITY has always existed in the world; it is as old as the miseries of human life. Whether this virtue is more active and more general in our day than in any preceding period is a question of history. It is not so clear that we sympathise more deeply with the afflicted and the unfortunate than our ancestors, or that humanity has now reached a perfection it never before attained. It is easy to see in this our day an excessive pride, and all the hideous offspring of which pride is the fruitful parent. The cup of misery is drunk now as always, but there exists also, unquestionably, in the present, a spirit of philanthropy as wide-spread and as active as in any former age. Indeed, it is fair to acknowledge that never has legislation been more strongly marked by the beneficent principle than at this moment. We live in a time when the dread sentence of penal servitude, pronounced in our High Courts of Justice, does but bind the felon to an apprenticeship, which is designed to prepare him for an honest life. The convict sent to jail, passes into a training establishment, conducted on benevolent principles. More than this, the law takes under its protection even the brute creation. It is an indictable offence for man to ill-use any of his domestic animals.

Then the benevolent institutions, supported at the public charge, and by private contributions, are numerous beyond example. There is a charity for the hungry, and a charity for the naked. There is a charity for "the maimed, the lame, and the blind," but the cry of hunger and nakedness, of pain and of sorrow is hushed in death, while the cry of the lost soul will be heard for ever. Hence, the charity which regards the soul or the part of man that is immortal, excelleth that which regards the part of him that is mortal, as far as light excelleth darkness. Now, there are eight hundred millions of Pagans, or eight out of every thirteen of the human race who have souls to be saved, and yet never heard of the Saviour, who redeemed them, nor of His holy Church! How incomparably divine, therefore, in the comparison, is the charity which has for its object the conversion of these millions, whose souls have been purchased by the Blood of the Lamb?

When the great apostle of the Gentiles, in the round of his missions, reached Troas, he became sorely distressed as to the future scene of his labours. One night, while praying earnestly for light, he had a vision, in which he saw a Macedonian on the opposite shore, beckoning him with imploring gesture to cross the circling waters of the intervening sea. He thought he heard a voice, coming to him from this apparition, to hasten to Macedonia, and preach there the faith of Jesus Christ. He thought he heard this voice breaking in upon the stillness of the night, and it seemed to him the voice of God, to which his heart beat in grateful and joyous response. Rising up he sought his sleeping companions, Silas, Timothy, and Luke, and waking them, they set sail directly for the shore to which they had thus been miraculously invited:—" And as soon as he had "seen the vision, immediately we sought to go into Macedonia, being assured that God had called us to preach the Gospel to them. And sailing from Troas we came with a straight course to Samothracia, and the day following to Neapolis."* Here is a touching example of the promptitude with which the heart of St. Paul bounded to the call of hapless Pagans of his time.

It was the same charity that made our own Ireland, in the first spring of her faith, send forth from her schools and monasteries a noble army of missionaries. Their preaching won to Christ the souls of those Pagan hordes, wild, fierce, and brutal, who poured in upon the countries of Europe, like the tide of a raging sea, burying under its great waves the civilization of the old Roman Empire. We do not know for certain the precise time—it is so long ago—when our forefathers first settled in this Island. But, we do know for certain that they came, long before the Christian era, from the East.

They had, no doubt, their faults, but they carried with them a noble nature. They were a high-spirited and brave people. Frank, hospitable, generous, confiding, affectionate, they were full of chivalrous attachment to their Princes and Bards, passionately fond of adventure, and devoted to poetry and the kindred arts. They were lively, witty, buoyant, seldom cast-down, and never broken

---

* Acts xvi. 10, 11.

by misfortune. Above all they were distinguished by their keen appreciation of intellectual excellence and profound reverence for the traditions of their race. Such was the Celtic character in the olden time, and such has it remained to the present day. It was a fitting soil for the seed of the Gospel, planted by St. Patrick. Never did a people become so rapidly and so thoroughly Catholic. Churches almost innumerable, sprung up at the bidding of the Apostle, and religious houses were filled with crowds of fervent contemplatives, amongst whom were the sons and daughters of the noblest in the land. In these monastic cities, as they have been called, sanctity and science found a home together; the students in letters and arts were counted by the thousand, whilst day and night a hymn of praise ascended without intermission to the throne of the Host High, It pleased Heaven to add to these marvellous favours the commission to teach :—" Go teach all nations, baptizing them in the name of the Father, and of the Son, and of the Holy Ghost." And forth went our Apostles on their mission, and though the field was rugged and inhospitable, it yielded to their industry. St. Columba led a heroic band to evangelize Scotland and Northumbria. Others crossing the seas, landed in Flanders, and took their course southward A blaze of light followed them along the Rhine, and to the East through the black forest of Germany, and into Austria to the South of the Danube. They penetrated as far as the extreme points of Italy and Spain, reaping everywhere a rich harvest of souls in these fair lands.

Thus Ireland achieved the most splendid of her ancient glories. But far more precious in the sight of the Lord is this charity when it is directed to the household of the faith —to the poor Christian pilgrims, worried and dispirited by the long conflict with sin. This is the compassionate and encouraging charity which "never falleth away, whether prophecies shall be made void, or tongues shall cease, or knowledge shall be destroyed."* It is in short the charity which sobers the reprobate in his mad career, softens the heart of the sinner to penitence, and is most perfect when it begins at home. It was by a marvellous zeal in the cause of this charity—the highest and noblest form of charity—that Ireland, in this, the second spring of her faith, has made her best conquests in the prosecution of her ancient and divine commission to teach. The zeal for saving souls is strong amongst us. Courageous priests and holy bishops from Ireland, like those of bygone times, are now doing the work of the ministry, wherever they are most needed.

It is painful to dwell upon the sad necessity that for many a year has forced our poor people to

---

* Corinth. xiii. 8.

leave all that is near and dear to them at home, to seek a livelihood in strange lands. But there is one thing which neither oppression nor hunger has been able to wrest from them—their faith. This is an inheritance preserved in the sanctuary of their own innocent homes, amidst perils and persecutions, the blackest that have ever disgraced any power, and this priceless treasure they have carried with them into their exile. But, as human nature is weak, the lamp of faith must be fed, otherwise it is in danger of being easily extinguished. Hence, in the early stages of the Irish exodus, when our Catholic people found themselves far away amongst the strangers, and entirely destitute of the saving ministrations of their religion, the lamp of their faith began to flicker. No longer the sounds of the village chapel bell proudly swelling up the glens and over the green hills of native land, are heard on the Sunday morning. The Sunday's Mass is no more for them, nor the priest in his snow-white robes to give them Communion at the altar-rails. Then, on the week-days there is no priest to advise them in doubt, or to minister to them in sickness and in sin. Thus the years come and go without the practice of their religion. At last the day comes round when the parents are seized with their last illness. In the presence of death the early memories of home come back, the spark of faith is kindled from its smouldering embers, and beseechingly they call for a priest, but there is none for them. Oh! the utter desolation of that dreadful hour! These unhappy parents have no priest to prepare them to meet their Judge. They die, and their last gasp is a shriek to heaven for mercy and forgiveness. Then it was that many a great penitent in the trackless wood and lonely valley of far-off lands wrote home, in terror of an unprovided death, for an Irish priest to come to save them. The heart of Catholic Ireland was wrung by this sorrowful message, and it was felt that missionaries must be sent, but missionaries could not be found.

In the meantime, the sons of these fathers and mothers grew into manhood, and the daughters into womanhood, without having once knelt before an altar or a priest. All the strengthening grace of the Sacraments, and all the fostering care of the priest they had lost. They had not the active agency of the Irish missionary to preserve their hearts from the seductive influence of the passions, and the lamp of their faith went out because they did not feed it. This melancholy news came also home in the second quarter of this century. It was announced over and over again personally and by letter that the children of Irish emigrants were to be found in large numbers amongst the various Protestant sects, simply because there were no Irish Missionaries among them to keep their faith alive. No later than a few weeks ago the distinguished Bishop of a foreign diocese told us at All Hallows that he knew in his parts the children of Irish parents, and most certainly with Irish Catholic names, hating the Catholic religion with a most bitter hatred, in the ranks of the Methodists and other Protestant denominations! And the famous Dr. England, Bishop of Charleston, has left it on record that there are thousands of persons in America alone, the descendants of Irish, who belong to the innumerable sects to be found in that country, who would now be Catholic had they been followed thither by their priests. No man could speak more truly of this lamentable fact, for no man could feel it more keenly than Dr. England. He was the son of an Irish father, whose terrible sufferings for the faith proved how dearly he loved it. One who knew him well thus wrote :—" More than " forty-five years have passed away since a man, " then about sixty years of age, led me into a " prison, and showed me the room in which he " had been confined during upwards of four " years, in consequence of the injustice to which " the Catholics of Ireland were subjected in those " days of persecution. On the day that he " was immured his wife was seized by fever, " the result of terror; whilst she lay upon her

" bed of sickness she and her family were dis-
" possessed of the last remnant of their land and
" furniture; she was removed to the house of a
" neighbour to breathe her last under a stranger's
" roof. Her eldest child had completed his
" seventeenth year a few days before he closed
" her grave. Two younger brothers and two
" younger sisters looked to him as their only sup-
" port. He endeavoured to turn his education to
" account. It was discovered that he was a *Papist*,
" as the law contumeliously designated a Roman
" Catholic, and that he was guilty of teaching
" some propositions of the Sixth Book of
" Euclid to a few scholars, that he might be able
" to aid his father and support his family. Infor-
" mations were lodged against him for this viola-
" tion of the law, which rendered him liable to trans-
" portation. Compassion was taken upon his
" youth and misfortunes, and instead of proceed-
" ing immediately to the prosecution, an opportu-
" nity was given him of swearing before the Pro-
" testant Bishop that he did not believe in the
" doctrines of Transubstantiation, of Penance, and
" of the Invocation of Saints; and the certificate
" of the Prelate would have raised a bar to his
" prosecution. The youth knew no principle of
" his Church which could excuse his perjury. He
" escaped and fled into the mountains, where he re-
" mained for more than a year, subsisting upon

"the charity of those to whose children he still
"communicated the rudiments of learning, but in
"the most painful anxiety as to the state of his
"father, brothers, and sisters.

"The declaration of American indepen-
"dence, and the successful resistance of the
"Colonists, having produced some mitigation
"of the persecutions which the Catholics
"endured, this fugitive returned by stealth to
"the city (Cork), and was enabled to under-
"take the duties of a land surveyor, to have
"his parent liberated, his family settled—and
"he became prosperous."

The brave man described here was the father of the Bishop of Charleston, and that Dr. England should note with sorrow, as he has done, the falling-off of the children of Irish emigrants in America from the faith is, as I have remarked, the best evidence of the truth of this lamentable fact.

In the presence of such appalling spiritual destitution of our expatriated countrymen, what Irish Catholic heart could remain unmoved? The cry of this spiritual famine, though mitigated, did not soon cease as time wore on. The Bishop of Natchez, Miss., U.S.; in October, 1859, wrote to the President of All Hallows in these words:—"I am now
"one hundred and twenty miles from any

"priest. The nearest one, who was to have
"accompanied me, I was obliged to leave at
"his residence, because there was some sick-
"ness in the neighbourhood. It will be ten
"days yet before I get to where there is a
"priest. Last week I said the '*De Profundis*'
"on the graves of some ten or twelve
"Catholics, in one place, not one of whom had
"a priest at his dying bed. Some of them
"had not seen a priest for three or four years."

Again in the February of the following year
he wrote :—" After I wrote to you from
"Houston last October, I heard of some Irish
"Catholics living far out of my intended line
"of travel. I went to look for them, and
"reached some. The others I could not get
"to without failing in my appointments. I
"baptized children four years old, who had
"never been seen by a priest, and blessed
"marriages which had been made three years
"ago before a magistrate for want of a priest.
"There were other cases of the same kind
"among those whom I could not reach." The
need still continues, although not, perhaps, to
the extent mentioned by the Bishop of Natchez.
And thus it happened that there arose a great cry
for Irish missionaries to keep the faith active among
the sons and daughters of poor Ireland in foreign
countries.

To meet this pressing need a great effort was demanded. It meant in the first place that the Lord of the vineyard would whisper into the ears of many a generous soul among our Catholic youth, the summons :—" Go ye also into my vineyard," and thus command them to make the painful sacrifice of " leaving home and brethren and sisters, and father and mother, for His name's sake, to earn a hundred fold and life everlasting." True, God did inspire many to make this painful sacrifice at the time. Catholic parents in this country readily offered to the holy cause their sons, who were in large numbers willing to give up all that is nearest and dearest in life to prepare themselves to go forth and dry the tears of their perishing countrymen. By a miracle God could furnish those pious and generous youths at once with the learning and training necessary to discharge their sacred duties. Then His angels could transport them to their distant missions, and when there He could send ravens to feed them as He did His prophets. But, He has committed to human hands the long and expensive education of His missionaries. Many years of careful study and discipline in an ecclesiastical college are necessary to teach the young missionary the form of sound words, before he can instruct others unto salvation. Before he can preach the Gospel in foreign parts he must also get there, and in many cases be supported there. To organize the human agencies, necessary for this formidable and complicated machinery, a man was needed possessing a deep mine of religious fervour, good ability, and great energy. God raised up this man, and he was Father Hand, founder of the Catholic Foreign Missionary College of All Hallows!

CHAPTER II.

A SCENE OF SOFT BEAUTY AND DARK SHADOWS.

CONTENTS.—The Inner not less than the Public Life of Father Hand to be Studied—Oldcastle, County Meath—Father Hand's Childhood—An Irish Eviction—Father George Leonard, the Pastor of Oldcastle—Father Hand's Family—The Rev. Robert Plunket lay Concealed in the Caves and Mountains of his Parish by Day, and did all the Duties of his Ministry by Night—Reflections of Dr. Doyle, Bishop of Kildare and Leighlin, on Dr. Gallagher, one of his Predecessors in 1737--Direful Condition of the Catholic Church in the Middle of the Eighteenth Century.

THE name of Father Hand is familiar to the generation now living. The blessed work of which he was the originator and the head, furnishes a theme for one of the brightest pages in the history of Christian charity. He was the Apostle of that divine mission which carried the message of salvation to his countrymen, who were forced to seek bread in the lands of the stranger. Hence his influence has been felt in the East and West Indies, in Australia, in America, North and South, and in more than one part of the British Isles. He remembered the glory that haloes around the path of Ireland in the first fervor of her faith. He followed the career of St. Columba, and Columbanus, of Killian, Cataldus, and the other celebrated missionaries, who made the moral desert of most of the Continent of Europe, bloom with Christian virtues. He studied closely all this, and though obscure, penniless and alone, he accomplished a result which, under God, lives to attest the divine Mission of the Sacred Isle.

Father Hand was, therefore, a public man. In examining the lives of such men, we are always anxious to know something of their private life. But Father Hand was one of those who broke suddenly upon the world, whose character strikes one by some strongly marked features. Now, these features or characteristics are not the growth of a day. They have been gradually developed in that earlier period of life which passed un-observed. Hence when his deeds now make him interesting we are all naturally curious about his early days in which the beginnings were laid. Nor is this curiosity confined to his early career, but extends itself to his inner life. It seeks to penetrate into the very sanctuary, if I may use the expression, of his existence. In many cases it may not be reverent to pry into the inner life of a great man; but his public acts do not often show the real man. Hence the world not unreasonably feels anxious to see how he bears himself in his domestic circle, free from the restraint, which the part he has taken before the gazing world necessitates.

In tracing the early life of Father Hand, it will be necessary to dwell on the years of his boyhood and point out those specialities of temper and character which marked him then. This has been made easy by his sister, Mrs. Tanham, in a narative she gave with native simplicity. It is pleasing to add, that her favourite son, with the spirit of his holy uncle strong upon him, passed some years ago from the halls of All Hallows, to minister to the spiritual wants of the miners in the recesses of the Pacific slopes under the jurisdiction of Bishop O'Connell, one of the most devoted Directors that ever served on the staff of All Hallows. Rev. Mr. Tanham is now one of a noble band of All Hallows' missionaries in that distant quarter of the Western Republic, who have to discharge the duties of their sacred ministry, under severe physical pain. By unfrequented paths too often, through woods and over prairies, crossing rivers, or stealing along precipices, they have to travel day by day seeking the wanderer and opening a door to the penitent. Often without a bed on which to repose at night, they snatch a few hours' sleep on the bare ground, only to resume their weary course on the morrow. To the mother of one of the youngest of these most laborious missionaries, and sister of Father Hand, is due most of what has been necessary to point out those traits of character in the boy which developed into the man.

Father Hand passed his childhood amidst the rich pastures of County Meath. He was born at Bolies, near *Oldcastle,* in August, 1807, and while yet very young was living with his parents further on from Oldcastle, at Stonefield, which they then occupied. No more fitting place for stimulating the germ of deep piety, which the boy without doubt possessed, could be found. The din of the outer world may be said never to enter this peaceful retreat. The distant noise of the city or the hum of active industry never invades its sacred calm. So great is the stillness of the place, that to use the words of an eloquent writer :—
" One is lifted up as it were out of the turmoil of
" the world into some planetary paradise, into
" some such place as the Apostle was invited, when
" the Voice said, 'Come up hither.' "

Then the beauty of the landscape quickens and elevates the love of meditation and prayer, which springs from the solemn stillness of the seclusion. There are lowlands stretching far into the horizon, and on these broad acres not a living thing to be seen, except herds of cattle. To relieve the monotony of this great flat, there are uplands, swelling into high hills and grassy knolls, on which flocks of sheep graze. These uplands terminate to the South, and South-East in an amphitheatre of the mountains of *Slieve-na Calliage* and *Slieve-Gullion,* at whose base repose the broad sparkling waters of Loughcrew, with their wooded banks.

But this scene of beauty is horridly disfigured by the presence of those sad surroundings which make Irish evictions so distressing. Here and there within the circle of this extensive prospect, there are broad spaces, strewn with the wreck of what were once happy homes. Dr. Nulty, the learned Bishop of the ancient diocese of Meath, whose native home is within view of those melancholy memories, has given an impressive account of what came under his own experience in one of the numerous evictions that make his county so barren of men, but the fruitful mother of flocks and herds. His Lordship's narrative is given in the brilliant pages of "New Ireland," Vol. 1 :—" Seven "hundred human beings were driven from their "homes on this one day. There was not a "shilling of rent due on the estate at the time, "except by one man. The Sheriff's assistants, "employed on the occasion to extinguish the "hearths and demolish the homes, of those honest, "industrius men, worked away with a will at their "awful calling until evening fall. At length an "incident occurred, that varied the monotony of "the grim and ghastly ruin, which they were "spreading all around. They stopped suddenly

"and recoiled, panic-stricken with terror, from two
"dwellings, which they were directed to destroy
"with the rest. They had just learned that typhus
"fever held these homes in its grasp, and had
"already brought death to some of their inmates.
"They therefore supplicated the agent to spare
"these houses a little longer, but he was in-
"exorable, and insisted that they should come
"down. He ordered a large winnowing-sheet to
"be secured over the beds on which the fever-
"victims lay—fortunately they happened to be
"delirious at the time—and then directed the
"houses to be unroofed cautiously and slowly. I
"administered the last sacraments of the Church
"to four of these fever-stricken victims next day,
"and save the above-mentioned winnowing-sheet,
"there was not then a roof nearer to me than the
"canopy of heaven. The scene of that eviction-
"day I must remember all my life long. The
"wailing of women, the screams, the terror, the
"consternation of children, the speechless agony
"of men, wrung tears of grief from all who saw
"them. I saw the officers and men of a large
"police-force, who were obliged to attend on the
"occasion, cry like children. The heavy rains,
"that usually attend the autumnal equinoxes,
"descended in cold copious torrents throughout
"the night, and at once revealed to the houseless
"sufferers the awful realities of their condition.

"I visited them next morning, and rode from place to place, administering to them all the comfort and consolation I could. The landed-proprietors in a circle all round, and for many miles in every direction, warned the tenantry against admitting them to even a single night's shelter. Many of these poor people were unable to emigrate. After battling in vain with privation and pestilence, they at last graduated from the workhouse to the tomb, and in little more than three years nearly a fourth of them lay quietly in their graves."

Such are the memories that now people the birth-place of Father Hand, and such the dark shadows that flit across the scene where he caught his passionate fondness for the beauties of nature. After his ordination he paid a visit to Woodville, which his father had just taken, and after examining the place all round, he rushed back into the house with a face lighted up, and warmly expressed his satisfaction with its scenery. When he came here to Drumcondra, though he gave himself hardly any time to saunter on its wooded slopes, or walk into the deep recesses of the Green Lanes, he felt their charms. Indeed his heart seemed to expand every year with the beauties of the early summer. He was up betimes to listen to the songs of birds, he rejoiced to contemplate

the flowers expanding into their infinite variety of colours, and to gaze on the greenness of the carpet which covered the winding landscape. A remarkable testimony of his cultivated taste in this respect has been given by one who was present at his burial in the College grounds:—
"We have never," says the writer, "witnessed "anything more beautiful than the procession "to the grave. The day was a heavenly one, "and there is no place where summer puts "on a deeper fascination than in All Hallows. "The fields so green and fresh—the trees so varied "and so rich in foliage—the walks so pleasingly "disposed and so admirably kept—reflected the "well-directed mind and great solicitude of the "man who is now no more."

And great, indeed, was Father Hand's solicitude for the neatness and arrangement of the grounds. Tastes like this, which are the graces of character, had their growth in Father Hand from the admiration he acquired in tender years for nature, when clothed in the beauties of opening summer. It was here also, in the solitude of the plain, in the shadows of venerable trees, he learned those lessons which saints have ever read in Nature's Book. Here he laid deeper and deeper the foundations of his faith; here he matured the practice of prayer which was his companion and stay all the days of his short but eventful life.

His family was an ancient one and highly respected. They were of that noble stock who in dark and penal days sealed the faith with their sufferings. Rev. George Leonard, the late pastor of Oldcastle, was during his long tenure of that important charge, a model of simplicity and zeal. No pastor ever lived more in the love and respect of his people, and deservedly, for he prayed and felt for all, and for none more than for him whom he always mentioned as "My beloved disciple, the "pious, the humble, the talented Father "Hand." He has informed us on this matter, for referring to Father Hand, he says:—"His "father was a near relative to the late Dr. "Plunkett of this diocese, so that he "seems to have inherited sanctity from his "birth." Then we are told all about the Plunketts: —"Robert Plunkett, the celebrated pastor of Kil- "bride and Castlecor, and candidate for the see of "Kilmore, at a time when the Catholic religion "was a crime, and the Catholic priesthood a felony, "was born here. The brightest feature in his "testimonials for that high office was, that in the "worst of times he was always at his post, and "never an exile. He was concealed in the caves, "and rocks, and mountains of his parish by day, "and doing all the duties of his ministry by night. "Oliver Plunkett, the last martyr of the Irish

"Church—the man whose merits were such as to "stem the rivers of Irish blood, which coursed in "torrents from 1641 to 1691—was also born here. "Why do I mention the names of these two great "men? To leave posterity to determine whether "Robert Plunkett or Oliver Plunkett could confer "greater benefits on the world than the great, the "good, the pious, the humble Father Hand."

Such was the family of the Plunketts to whom the founder of All Hallows belonged. The Rev. Robert Plunkett, the pastor of Kilbride and Castlecor, "at a time when the Catholic religion was a crime, and the Catholic priesthood a felony," lay concealed "in the caves, and rocks, and mountains of his parish by day, and doing all the duties of his ministry by night!!" To form a proper estimate of the sufferings of the Catholic bishop or priest like the Rev. Robert Plunkett, who was fortunate enough to save his head in the middle of the eighteenth century, there is a good instance in the Right Rev. James Gallagher, well-known as the author of many beautiful sermons in the Irish tongue, which are pronounced by competent judges to be fully equal to Fenelon's finest discourses. He was consecrated Bishop of Raphoe in 1721, and sixteen years afterwards translated to the diocese of Kildare and Leighlin. He is sketched in the popular life of Dr. Doyle by Mr. Fitzpatrick in these terms:—"Shortly after the "consecration of Dr. Doyle," writes the author, "he was accompanied on his visitation to the "obscure village of Allan by the present parish "priest of Kildare. 'Do you see those wretched "mud-walls?' observed the latter. 'They are the "ruins of the Episcopal palace of one of your pre- "decessors, who there, in penal days, ate the bread "of tribulation and drank the waters of adversity. "Although an active labourer in the diocese, he "was never without some pious youths in the house "with him, whom he instructed in Greek and "Latin, and theology, previous to sending them "to Paris for ordination. Thus did this good man, "almost in sight of the gibbet, continue to keep "up this scanty supply of pastors for the poor of "Kildare and Leighlin. His bones lie beneath "yonder uninscribed grave.' Dr. Doyle was "visibly affected. He remained silent for some "time, and then broke out into a train of musing "such as this :—'What must be my reflections at "hearing of the danger and labours of these "good men, and what a reproach to my own sloth, "and sensuality, and pride? They of whom the "world was not worthy, and who went about in "fens, and morasses, and in nakedness, and thirst "and hunger, and watching and terror, will be "witnesses against me for not using to the best "advantage the blessings which their merits have "obtained from God for their children.' Else-

" where he says :—'The Catholic Bishop of this "diocese, in a shed, built of mud and covered with "rushes, on the verge of the Bog of Allan—the "refuge of a man not inferior in mind or virtue to "Fenelon—instructed youth with his own tongue, "and shared with them the crust which he had first "watered with the tears of affliction.'" Here is a picture, and in no particular overdrawn of what may be conceived to be the condition of the pastor of Kilbride and Castlecor. But since the history of a man cannot be duly estimated without reference to the time in which his lot was cast, it seems useful to inquire what the state of the Irish Church was when this good pastor appeared, whom Father George has so happily united in blood with his own "beloved disciple."

We have seen how Ireland, in the fresh ardour of her conversion, won the most splendid of her ancient glories in the divine commission to teach. This happened at a time when she carried not only the light of the Gospel but the light of science and civilization into the barbarous parts of Europe. It was then her sons preached the faith, and revived literature and arts long buried under the wreck of barbarian invasions. Young men flocked from distant lands to our schools, and stayed with us to learn the sacred sciences and other polite learning. When they were leaving they bade a blessing on the land, and published on their way back and at home that Ireland was in truth a land of scholars and of saints. And so our country came to be called the " Isle of Saints," a name which has lived ever since in the traditions and histories of European nations. For more than two centuries the glory of the Irish Church was undimmed, but then came a change. Tribes of savages, whose occupation was war and rapine, landing on our shores, swept suddenly like a storm over the land, devastating and plundering as they went, and before men could recover from the surprise, they were back to their ships with their spoils. By degrees these freebooters built strong castles on the sea-coast and afterwards others in the interior of the country, whence they plied their infamous trade. It was an hour of affliction for the Church, since her treasures excited the cupidity of this ferocious race. At length our forefathers, gathering together their strength, drove the robbers from post to post, so that the vanquished sent home for help, and presently their countrymen came in swarms, for their name was legion. But after a long war they were annihilated in a great battle by the sea, and that was the last of the Danes in Ireland.

Another two centuries passed away, and there came a new race of strangers. Our own dissensions brought them hither, and gave them a footing when they came. They had many noble qualities, the Anglo-Normans had, but their motto was *divide and rule*, and they were skilled in their craft. Being a calculating race, and bold withal in action, and unscrupulous and cruel, they were able to perpetuate the divisions they found amongst us, and even to multiply them.

In the centuries that followed, the Church often put on her mourning weeds. She had to weep over shrines that were stripped of their beauty; she had to weep over the wrongs inflicted by these strangers on those whom she cherished; and she had to weep, alas! more than once over the follies and faithlessness of her own children. But she was not without consolation, for the strangers still caressed her for their mother, and her erring sons most commonly came back to shed tears of penance at her feet.

Protestantism having made for itself a home in England, crossed over here to Ireland, backed by iron hands and fierce passions. The Catholic instinct of the Irish people shrank from it as from something foul. It was thrust upon them; they pushed it back, and then began the age of martyrs —the age in which the Prophets were scourged in the synagogues, and the blood of the priests spilled between the temple and the altar. What a vision of suffering rises up now before us! Armies let loose upon unopposing and unarmed peasants, prescriptions of entire races, treacheries, imprisonments, private executions without number. These are the characteristic traits of the reigns of Elizabeth and the First James of England. Tracing down the red track we come upon hordes of armed men, with the instincts of tigers, beating up and down the country. They had been exercised for years in spilling the blood of their weaker foes in Scotland, and ended by the murder of their king, and now they are over to Ireland to push on their unhallowed pursuit. But it is better to draw a veil over the butcheries and ruin wrought by Cromwell and his followers. A time followed when a certain King of England, driven by his son-in-law from his throne, took refuge among his Irish subjects. They gathered round him, and made a gallant defence—first for their exiled king, and then for their own liberty. The war was closed by the well-known "Treaty of Limerick," in which, among other things, it was solemnly stipulated that the Catholics should henceforward be allowed to profess and practise their religion without molestation. This done, the Irish troops disbanded; some went to their own homes, but most of them went abroad, where their valour reaped a rich harvest of glory, and to this day their name and blood fill the highest posts in the armies of the first Powers in Europe. These brave men once gone from the country, we know how it fared with the guarantee of our religious liberties. Adventurers of the Williamite army, joining adventurers of a previous period, formed themselves into a strong faction, who seized upon all the offices of the Administration. They brought together a gang which, under the name of an Irish Parliament, tore the Treaty of Limerick in pieces, and enacted against Catholics the infamous Penal Code. And so by this "elaborate contrivance of oppression" was literally fulfilled the words of the sad dirge in which the Prophet laments that " the ways of Sion mourn, " because there are none that come to the solemn " feast; all her gates are broken; her priests sigh, " her virgins are in affliction, and she is oppressed " with bitterness. Her adversaries are become her " lords, her enemies are enriched, her children are "led into captivity before the face of her oppressor."[*]

This was the direful condition to which the infamous Penal Code had reduced the Catholic Church when the kinsman of Father Hand, the celebrated pastor of Kilbride and Castlecor, the Rev. Robert Plunkett, appeared.

---

[*] Lamentations i. 4.

CHAPTER III.

A MOTHER'S PICTURE AND A FIRST COMMUNION.

CONTENTS.—Young Hand's affection for his Mother—His First Communion—He maintained an intimate union with his Divine Lord, by going to Confession and to the Altar every Month—He fasted the Wednesdays and Fridays of every Week, and every day in Lent—He had a tender compassion for the wants of his poorer neighbours—He was neglecting himself while ceaselessly guarding the comforts of others.

YOUNG Hand ripened early into one of the most gentle and affectionate of natures. He would join heart and soul in those innocent amusements of boys, but shrank with horror from what are known as their *wild sports*. As might be supposed, his amiable sensitiveness, while it drove him from the rude sports of boys, drew him closer to a loving and sympathetic mother. Of all her children, and she was blessed with many, John had the first place in her regard, and no wonder! For not only was he most lovable from his goodness and gentleness, but there was a sweet gravity, even a dignity, in his manner, which was most remarkable in one so young. And he returned the mother's love with deep affection, for she was the only member of his immediate family to whom he communicated his intention of establishing a College at Dublin for the Foreign Missions. But there is abundant evidence to show that this affection for his mother, even after he had wrenched his heart from home and all its endearing affections, seemed to sink deeper every day into his soul. And in this he exhibited one of the most fascinating qualities that go to make up a beautiful character. For who is it that is not forced to kneel and weep when the thoughts of a mother's love crowd upon his mind? Who can recall without emotion from earliest years the words that fell from the lips most dear to us, the happy memories of childhood and home?

It was at the knee of his sympathising mother young Hand learned those beautiful prayers in which he held sweet converse with God. She taught him, as yet a child, to lisp the sacred names which he fondly remembered in his use of frequent aspirations. And what more beautiful aspiration than to invoke the adorable name of Jesus—that name above all other names—that hallowed name at the sound of which every knee in heaven, and in earth, bends in humble adoration! And when in the moments of our sorrow and trial we call upon *Jesus* the Son, we must not forget *Mary* the Mother—she who brought Him forth in a cold stable—shared all His privations, and finally saw Him expire a bleeding victim for the sins of men. These were the sacred names—Jesus and Mary—which, as yet a child, Father Hand learned at his mother's knee, and which all through life were in his heart as well as on his lips.

He was now nine years of age when he gratified his mother immensely by the announcement of his intention to make his first communion, which he had long put off from an over-scrupulous sense of his unworthiness. In due time the day of the first communion for the children of the parish was appointed by Father George, who, even at this early age, began to like the boy, for those qualities which developed into that broad charity, which is one of the wonders of the Irish Church. Now, that the day of his first communion had been fixed—the day, which he had been looking forward to so long, his sense of unworthiness increased. But, the fond mother, who had been observing the nervous oppression of her son, found a thousand opportunities of conveying to him some elation of spirits. When the day arrived, though he had to walk some distance, he was in the chapel with his mother long before the service. Father George, then, and for many years Curate to his aged and venerable uncle, the Abbé MacDermott, had, during his College course, studied at the feet of a master, distinguished alike for profound learning, piety, and the true ecclesiastical spirit. This was the illustrious Dr. Doyle, afterwards Bishop of Kildare and Leighlin. The pupil, like the master, had a tender care for the little ones of the flock, and with reason, seeing that our Lord pleaded their cause, when He said on a memorable occasion :—" Suffer the little children, "and forbid them not to come to Me : for the "kingdom of heaven is for such." * Father George, therefore, invested the first communion of the children of the parish with all the solemnity he could command. Hence, on the present occasion, he was in the Church, or more properly in the Chapel, because of its modest pretensions, to greet with genial smile and reverential whisper the children as they trooped into their places. They felt at once the solemnity of the occasion, and as they looked upon him, they read in the gentle movement of his lips, the sentiments which ought to penetrate their little hearts. Then, as the hour for Mass was approaching, the good priest had all the decorations brought out and arranged on the altar. He did this in order that the children might see in the spotless linen, in the lights and flowers, the immaculate purity of soul required from them to receive their Lord worthily. And among all that throng of innocents not one felt more sincerely than young Hand that his soul ought to be as pure as the gold of the chalice, and as spotless as the altar linen. He believed

---

* Matthew xix. 14.

that his thoughts, resolutions, and petitions ought to be infinitely more bright than the flowers and lights of the sanctuary. That first communion was truly a love-feast to him, and when roused from his prolonged thanksgiving by his exulting mother, and was leaving the chapel-door, " he "stood to take one longing, lingering look," at the scene of what he always remembered as his greatest joy.

But, as this first communion was his greatest joy, it was also the stay of that salutary fear, of never doing, or saying, or thinking anything, calculated to endanger that purity of soul, and that strength of resolution, which were imparted to him now at the altar-rails. In this he shared the fears of the greatest saints, and it is as the fear which one experiences, who from our port :—"goes down " to the sea in ships, doing business in the great " waters." In the voyage of life there are many dangers to faith and morals. John Hand was keenly alive to this, and in order to avoid them he took care to keep the course he resolved on in making his First Communion. On the eve of the first Sunday in every month, he went to the chapel to confession, and the following day in the early morning he received holy communion. Then the whole of that day, except a few minutes for a hurried breakfast in a friend's house hard by, he spent in the chapel. For hours before communion he was to be seen kneeling on the damp floor, pouring out the feelings of his unworthiness for so great a dignity, and begging his Lord to make his soul pure for the reception of the great sacrament of love. And when he approached the altar, oh the burning love within, and the rapt recollection without! Then the time of thanksgiving he gave to protracted communing with God, whom he had just received.

Fasting is another powerful help to avoid the rocks and quick-sands of our earthly voyage, and young Hand fasted the Wednesdays and Fridays of every week, and every day in Lent. Of all the circumstances mentioned in the life of our divine Lord, none strikes us with so much wonder—none more clearly evinces his ardent love for man's salvation, than that connected with His fast " of " forty days and forty nights." The Divine voice was heard in the midst of assembled thousands proclaiming Him to be the well-beloved son of the Father, pleasing in His sight, and through whom alone, full atonement coul l be made to His offended justice. It was then :—" Jesus was led by the "Spirit into the desert, to be tempted by the devil !" Thus He who came down from heaven to wipe out the handwriting of sin that was against us, came also as our model. In the gracious designs of Omnipotent goodness, the office of Redeemer included that of guide and instructor. We see in this circumstance but a portion of that great system of instruction, carried out in our regard by the Blessed Saviour in every act of His mortal life. This was a part of that system of man's redemption —that sublimest conception of Divine love, derived and worked out by an all-good Jesus. This is the idea alluded to by the great St. Augustine, when he said :—" Jesus Christ wished to show us that " as *He*, while on earth, was exposed to the attacks " of the tempter, *we* could not hope to escape, and " that as *He* conquered, so *we*, by following His " bright example, might have a share in the same " glorious victory." Young Hand fasted rigorously, and by this weakening of the sensual appetite he was able to note accurately the signs in the sky on his voyage to the grave, and secure himself from striking against the rocks and sands, which render the course so perilous.

He had tender compassion for the wants of his poorer neighbours, and experienced the sincerest gratification in giving them happiness. A very pleasing instance of this charming feature in his character may be gathered from an incident related of him at this time by his sister, Mrs. Tanham. The wives and children of the cottiers from the neighbourhood came to his mother's dairy to buy their daily supply of milk. The sight of these poor people, struggling with their pence for the mere necessaries of life, stirred his compassionate nature to its very depths, and made him anxiously seek some opportunity of showing these creatures how he felt for them. It came about in this way. The good mother had the generous custom of giving milk gratuitously to the people on certain days in the year, and to turn this to his account the boy cleverly employed the influence which he derived from his mother's love. With her permission he was present to distribute the milk on these fixed days, and for those who could not come, he coaxed from the mother a good supply for each and carried it with his own hands to their cottages at a considerable distance.

This consideration for the wants of his neighbours was a fitting school to learn that simplicity of character, that thorough sympathy for the faithful poor, that enduring patience, that habit of cheerful assistance which characterized him through life. And this habit of seeking to afford pleasure to others is one of the best preserved traditions of him in All Hallows. Here it has come down that while he was reckless to a degree in regard to any indulgence for himself, he was ceaselessly guarding the comforts of the humblest individual in the College. Thus he was lavish of furniture and fittings on the rooms of his colleagues, but in his own room :—

> "His down-bed a pallet— his trinkets a bead,
> His lustre—one taper that serves him to read;
> His sculpture—the crucifix nailed by his bed,
> His paintings—one print of the thorn-crowned head."

Again, though he wasted and wore himself away in the painful work of begging for the College, his colleagues never missed the sunshine from his brow. He never, even by remote hint, conveyed to them that they ought to share with him—their superior —that which must necessarily be the most oppressive business in the community. And so too with their faults—and who is it that has not faults? so far from characterizing them with the sting of personal remark, or expostulation, he did not show the slightest sign of having even noticed these faults. And yet he would be impatient, and demonstratively irritable with what was the most involuntary and apparent weakness in himself. He was, indeed, all sweetness and benevolence to those who had the happiness of being associated with him in his holy work, and could crowd all his terrible anxieties into his own mind, and cover it over with a happy smile, sooner than occasion one moment's pain even to those upon whom he ought to lean. In short, this delightful disposition of affording pleasure to others which I have endeavoured to point out, developed into the most remarkable feature of Father Hand.

CHAPTER IV.

THE YOUNG SHEPHERD IS INVITED OVER TO BETHLEHEM.

CONTENTS.—Young Hand had to walk some miles for his daily lesson—His father's notion of binding him to some mercantile employment—His persistent practice of prayer—His fondness for music—Convent of our Lady of Charity, High Park, Dublin—Mr. Hand is summoned by God to the service of the Sanctuary—His father's opposition—He is sent to a Classical School at Oldcastle for three years—His father insisted on his working on the farm before and after school—He enters the Seminary at Navan.

ABOUT twelve the boy was sent to school. Catholics at this time had not the school accommodation they now possess, and young Hand had therefore to walk a distance of some miles for his daily lesson. This, however, he held cheap in comparison with the knowledge for which he thirsted. He was not long in learning the rudiments, and his quick parts soon brought him under the favourable notice of the teacher. The scholars called him the "Master," regarding him with affectionate respect as superior to themselves.

For many years under this excellent teacher, the boy, Hand, could not fail to acquire that superior elementary education, which he undoubtedly possessed. Indeed so remarkable was his progress that the father, with but slender means and a large family, had a notion of securing his help by placing him in some mercantile employment. But—

> "All is best, though oft we doubt
> What the unsearchable *dispose*
> Of highest Wisdom brings about."

Or as Father George prophetically remarked:— "How sweetly divine Providence disposes of all "things? My shilling book premium found out "Father Hand! If I never gave premiums for "the best answering in the meaning of the "catechism, or the best answering in the lesson "from the 'Elevation of the Soul,' or 'Manning's "Moral Entertainments,' or 'Bourdaloue's "Spiritual Retreat,' which I read at vespers; "or for the best answering in the history of the "Bible, and in the history of the Church, per- "haps, Father Hand would never be as much "as heard of. I claim no merit for my share "in the education of this great and good man, "but I say with the Psalmist, 'Not to us, O "Lord, not to us; but to Thy name give "glory.'"

Young Hand, while thus laying the foundation of human learning, added considerably to the wisdom of the Saints which struck its roots down deep in his soul, the day of his first communion. These roots he watered by the persistent practice of prayer, and in this way kept the eyes of his heart from the transient and perishable things of the present, to fix them on the unchangeable goods of the future. At home he prayed every day, humbly, fervently and perseveringly, and gave nearly the whole of Sunday to devotions in the parish chapel. Then, returning in the late evening home, he never failed in gathering around him his brothers and sisters to read for them a chapter of some of those pious books he won from Father George in premiums, after which the whole family joined invariably in a long Rosary. He had a special love for Vespers, that beautiful evening song or service of the Catholic Church, and though his voice was not strong, its sweet tones added much to the effect of the Vesper hymn in which he took a principal part. He was fond of music, and the only distraction he found afterwards from his severe labours at Phibsboro', was in paying a visit some evenings to the house of the O'Reilly's of Ratoath, a family very dear to him, and among the first to open their purse liberally for his efforts in the cause of the Foreign Missions. He listened with the most demonstrative delight to the singing of Moore's melodies, and it is a pleasing reflection that the voice which then touched the chords of his thoroughly Irish heart, and made the strings of the instrument vibrate to her words, is now in the Convent of Our Lady of Charity, High Park, near Dublin. There this lady may be seen in the midst of that fervent sisterhood, in her simple habit of white serge, and on her breast, the well-known silver heart, on which is a figure of Him whose humble follower she is. Unknown to the world, but known to God, and for His sake, she is drying the tears of the penitent.

It was thus the young shepherd was spending his days and nights in innocence and prayer, when he heard the sweet music of heaven inviting him over to Bethlehem. Towards the beginning of the present century, from the better state of public opinion, and the fear of provoking the hostilities of a numerous community, persecution began to slacken its fires. When the priest said Mass in a hovel, or when he went to administer the sacraments to any of his flock, he was not molested, because these things were performed away from the sight of the Protestant eye. Hence the Catholics of Ireland did not build stately churches, rich in ornamental architecture, like those which now grace our island. Thank God, the altar is now free in the dear old land. If the charity of the

Irish race is patient, it is also kind. That love of God, which bore with such marvellous patience the fierce persecutions of so many generations, is now active in replacing the ruined altars of the ages of blood by new ones, more beautiful even than the old. Churches, remarkable in most instances for their beauty, have of late sprung up everywhere in Ireland—in the cities, in the villages, on the mountain-sides, and in the remote glens.

But towards the end of the last, or the beginning of the present century, our parish churches were built down in some secluded ravine, over the rude altar of rock or turf, where the Catholics used to hear Mass in the days of their mourning. They erected simple, bare chapels, without comfort or ornament. Of this class was the temple in which young Hand spent his Sundays and holidays in communion with God. He did not pray before an altar of marble. He saw not gold, nor precious stones, nor rich textures in silk, nor any of the costly things with which the Church loves to decorate the sanctuary. He gazed not on lofty arch or painted window, but his eyes rose from the bare walls, on to the plain ceiling, and thence to heaven. There was neither choir nor organ to carry him away in waves of solemn music. He heard but the symphony of the worshippers telling their beads, or the more subdued voice of the passing wind sobbing through the aged oaks.

This was the Bethlehem to which young Hand was now invited by the sweet music from heaven. It was the depth of winter, when everything around looked chilled and drooping. The greenness of the carpet, that covered the winding landscape, had almost disappeared. The mountains of *Slieve-na-Callagh* and *Sliev Gullion*, in the distance, wore their heavy crowns of snow, and all nature seemed to be shivering.

Through this changed and roughened scene our young shepherd went in haste to Bethlehem. Entering, he knelt down to offer his love and gratitude for this heavenly invitation, when the same voice from above fell upon his ears. He thought he heard the Angel announcing the tidings of great joy, that the new-born Saviour summoned him to the service of the Sanctuary. The summons struck a responsive chord in the breast of the young shepherd. He obeyed with wonderful faith, and though he found his divine Lord spurned out of doors, driven to take up His abode among beasts, he but loved Him the more for all this humiliation. Now, that he had been chosen to be " for Christ, an Ambas-"sador," he resolved to seek the humiliation of his Divine Master. Rising from his knees, he felt so transported with gratitude for this astounding favour

that he resolved not to lose a moment in hastening home and confiding the secret to his dear mother. She, having embraced her darling boy, thanked God, and then mentioned the father's intention of binding him to some business in which he could earn money. He listened to her gentle words, he looked into her streaming eyes, and falling on his knees with her hands held in his own, he cried in a voice, choked with emotion :—" Mother, you must speak for me." He beheld the familiar smile on her sweet face, and he felt in the tender pressure of her hand that his cause was safe. Accordingly, his purpose she was not long in conveying to her husband, and tried, with all her arts, to persuade him into consent, but without effect. He was a man of rugged disposition, and calling the son in a tone of much harshness, he addressed him thus:—
" The mother has been just speaking to me of your " wish, and this is my answer, that you begin to " help us at once. It is rough work here in the " farm, but you must do it, or serve your time to " some business, for there is a big family." Again the wife urged every argument in her power to soften the husband's resistance, but in vain. He was inexorable, until Father George stood before him.

It appears the worthy priest, after Catechism on Sundays, had a Bible and Church history-class for the more advanced children. On certain Sundays in the year a public examination was held in these subjects, and prizes given to those, who answered best. In all these public tests young Hand came off first, and thus he rose immensely in the estimation of Father George, who relates the fact in these words :—" To the History of the Bible and " the History of the Church, I added Cobbett's " History of the Reformation, and in every book " John Hand was leader, and fit to stand an exa- " mination in the full contents of every book I " named. If I made a small mistake, John Hand " was able and willing to correct me. The book " would be appealed to, and John was invariably " found to be correct." Clearly, Father George was now as fairly under the spell of the boy's capacity for learning, as he had been under that of his virtues. He made him companion in his walk on Sundays between the time for religious instruction and Vespers. In this way the good priest had ample opportunity of sounding his " beloved disciple's " character to its depths, and of observing that, while it was clear and transparent to the very bottom, it was so smooth in its motion as not to ruffle the surface or sully the purity of its waters. In one word, he found it to be a character shaped by God's own hand for the service of the altar, and in it he detected the germ of the meek and unaffected grace, which adorned his own career in the ministry. "I remember," says Father

George, "remarking at this time what a loss it "would be to bury such talent in the farm," and so the worthy pastor came to destine, in his own mind, his "beloved disciple" for the high and holy office, to which the boy had been so singularly invited by Heaven. " O the depth of the riches of " the wisdom and of the knowledge of God! How " incomprehensible are His judgments, and how un-" searchable His ways." We can therefore imagine easily the joy with which Father George, during one of their accustomed Sunday walks, listened to young Hand as he related the history of his heavenly call to the ministry! But this joy was changed into intense pain when the pious youth described his father's inflexible opposition, and the stern attitude he had assumed to the mother's earnest pleading. The "beloved disciple" was then comforted by a promise of the good priest's powerful influence in bringing over the father to their side. And the father did yield to his pastor's pressing solicitations, but with a bad grace. The son was sent to an academy, or grammar-school, in Oldcastle, on the condition that his mornings and evenings at home should be devoted to the general work of the farm. "When John "Hand," writes Father George, "was about sixteen "years old, his father consented with reluctance "to allow him to go to Mr. Molloy's Classical "School, on condition, however, that he would not

"lose a moment from his work. To this John
"readily agreed; and before school-hour and after
"his return home, he did more than any lad of his
"age would do in a day. Though in part of the
"harvest he would remain at home, and in spring
"he would do the same, he was always the leader
"of his class at school. He committed to memory
"a great portion of Homer and Cicero, and looked
"to the lexicon and dictionary for every word,
"and would not be losing his time in reading a
"translation."

For three years young Hand thus continued to cultivate the ancient classics. Father George also continued to grow warmer and warmer in his praise, while the remarkable progress of his gifted pupil inspired Mr. Molloy with admiration. Yet, all this time young Hand was breasting the waves of obstruction at home. The father set a higher value on the son's help in his own farm, than on his gleaning golden grain in the field of the ancient Greek and Latin authors. Hence he was ever severe in exacting from the boy a strict fulfilment of the hard conditions, on which he was allowed the luxury of Mr. Molloy's Academy. It happened that the young lad, in his great thirst for study, often violated the *bond* by stealing into some remote corner of the house to give himself to his all absorbing lessons. Thither the father came in search of him, but the son, who was always watching for the approach of the enemy, flung his books into a recess in the window, and escaped. The father, however, to chain him more effectually to his side, marked out what he was to do about the farm, before and after school. But, here again, John was equal to the occasion, for he turned his sweet disposition, which endeared him to his brothers and sisters, and made him a pet with the servants, into a means of inducing one now, and one again, to do the work the father had assigned to him.

At the end of three years, the father's opposition melted under the warm sunshine of John's patient and prayerful manner. One day he called the son, and in a voice broken with sobs spoke to him to this effect:—" My dear boy, I had hoped you " would be the support of your aged parents. I " had hoped to see you always here helping your " mother, and in the farm by my own side. But " Father George tells me you are the making of a " good priest—that God has called you to serve " Him at the altar. He says you are great at " the learning with Mr. Molloy, and I know " you are too close at the big books. He says " I must now send you to the Navan Seminary, " and the mother says so, too. I will do so, " but I cannot spare more than will pay for you

"as a day-boy. Your aunt has offered you a
"corner with herself, and I will do the rest. It
"will surely be hard on you, John, to walk the four
"miles from your aunt's to Navan every morning,
"and the same four miles back in the evening, but
"Father George says you are willing to do it.
"God bless you, then, my dear boy! I little
"thought we would have to part in this way, but
"you will think of your father, with his gray hairs,
"drudging in the farm here, and your poor mother
"looking after the work of the house."

CHAPTER V.

THE STING OF DEFEAT.

CONTENTS.—Mr. Hand's successful studies in Navan Seminary—He had to walk eight miles daily in going to and coming from the Seminary at Navan—Very Rev. Dr. M'Elroy, Vicar-General of Meath—Mr. Hand's victory in the competition for Maynooth was set aside—His year of dark disappointment at home—He was sent to Maynooth as Assistant-Bursar—Demonstration of hostility towards him—The virtue of Christian forgiveness —Mr. Hand's inner life in Maynooth.

A FEW days after the affecting interview with his father, described in the last chapter, young Hand was making his way, under quite a load of books, from the house of an aunt near Kells to the seminary, some four miles off. Pleased and unwearied, he glided under the shade of pendent woods, by rich meadows, yielding to the mowers' scythe, and fields, floating with waves of yellow corn. It was truly a rural paradise on this early harvest day, and out of it he passed into the straggling street of a provincial town, flanked by damaged houses or mud cabins, such as one could hardly expect to meet with in a smiling country. This is Navan, where at one end, may be seen *the Seminary*, and through its gloomy portals young

Hand entered to drink deep of the Pierian spring. This institution, opened in 1802, seems to have already grown old in the service of literature, but like the very ivy on the ruin, the wrinkles on its brow give it a venerable appearance. Stepping into an inner court, one is told to contemplate the *Palæstra*, on an elevated spot, reached by a stone stairs. Where are the sacred groves of Academus? They have not been transplanted, and it is well, for like the *Palæstra* they would suffer in the carriage. But the beauty of this ancient seat of learning is "within in golden borders." If not the very first, it was one of the first Seminaries, built in Ireland, after the repeal of the penal laws, and since then, it has been the cradle of a succession of learned and holy priests, who have given Meath a foremost place in the Irish Church.

Young Hand was nineteen when he came to Navan, and immediately he set vigorously to work. He was, however, a day-boy, and the interns affected to look down upon him, thinking in their foolish hearts that brains existed exclusively in money. They soon discovered their mistake, for the day-boy, John Hand, in very little time, "all his peers he did surpass," and continued to do so, during a brilliant curriculum of four years. Logic was the study of his fourth year, and young Hand's capacity for the tangled details of this abstruse branch, was not less conspicuous than what he showed in his long course of Latin and Greek classics and mathematics. The Very Rev. Dr. M'Elroy, parish priest of Tullamore, and Vicar-General of Meath, in his life a model of Evangelical zeal, and in his conversation a deep well of Ecclesiastical learning, recalls to mind how John Hand led the Logic class in the Seminary all through his fourth year, and this while he covered, day after day, his eight miles' journey, sometimes in the face of pelting rain and drifting snow! Often he saw him, coming into class, thoroughly drenched, and sitting in his scanty clothing, with hands, looking red and raw from the intense cold. "And yet," Dr. M'Elroy added, "Mr. 'Hand, though cold and wet in body was "keen in mind. With his manly but modest "bearing, and clear head, he was the cynosure of "all neighbouring eyes." No one can speak upon this matter with more authority than the accomplished Vicar-General of Meath, for he sat with Mr. Hand, though on a lower form, at Navan for three years, and from that time they became sincere friends.

These triumphs of "his beloved disciple" in the Seminary, were watched with great pride by Father George. He quite exulted in the news of every fresh victory, and always came to Stonefield in the tranquil evenings, to talk over these splendid successes with the old people. Mrs. Tanham recalls distinctly, even at this distance of time, the beaming, benevolent face of the good pastor as he sat recounting the pleasing intelligence to her rejoicing parents. Then, as Father George went back in the gloaming to his simple home—

"The children paused in their play to kiss the hand extended to bless them,
Reverend walked he among them, and up rose matrons and maidens,
Hailing his slow approach with words of affectionate welcome."

As Mr. Hand's fourth year in the Seminary was drawing to a close he became very anxious, since his name was down on the list of candidates for College. The Seminary had mainly to depend for its support on the fees of the intern students, and that they should have a preference in the competition for Maynooth, came to be the traditional policy of the institution. In this Father George, and "his beloved disciple" saw danger, and their fears proved to be well-grounded. The "little cloud" "as a man's hand" overspread the sky on the day of the competition, and though Mr. Hand won, his claim was made to give way to the traditional rights of the intern students. But, there was present on this occasion one who, in the exercise of his high office, presided at the oral examinations, and applauded Mr. Hand's superiority of parts with occasional bursts of acclamation. This was

Dr. Cantwell, late Bishop of Meath, and a Prelate of happy memory. In pronouncing his funeral panegyric some years ago, Dr. M‘Hale, the great Archbishop of the West, said :—"John Cantwell "appeared like a pillar of light on the mountain- "tops." Therefore, the late Bishop of Meath was no ordinary man, and this is why his appointment in 1830, met with so much public favour. One of his first acts was to take the chair in the Seminary at the examination of the candidates for Maynooth. His ripe scholarship, was, we saw, attracted and kindled into demonstrations of applause, by the facility with which Mr. Hand solved the difficulties proposed. But, afterwards in private council, when the Bishop urged the claims of his favourite, the authorities of the Seminary firmly objected in the interests of the institution committed to their care. " How did his Lordship expect to maintain the " Diocesan Seminary, if merit alone be taken into " account ?" This was the argument to which the Bishop had to yield in the present instance, but at the same time he pronounced his decision in language that became proverbial. He declared that in future, the alleged prescriptive rights of intern students shall prevail only, when there is a tie between candidates in the order of merit, or as his Lordship classically expressed it, *cæteris paribus.*

Mr. Hand was ordered home for another year,

and the announcement sank as iron into his soul. How could he face that home where he was expected coming with joyfulness from the harvest, carrying the sheaves which he sowed in the tears of the last four years? How could he encounter that anxious father, whose slender purse he had been draining in the past? If he now ventured to seek the home of his youth, that door where once the loving welcome of a mother greeted his approach, would be practically closed in his face. However, it would be to him a gratification to revisit the scenes where he spent his early days, and as no such opportunity might again occur, he directed his course towards native plains. Here, shut out from nearly every joy, he found consolation in examining, with the kind-hearted Father George, every spot with which some fond memory was associated. In this trying time he also stole over to Bethlehem often in the evenings, and found relief in prayer before his divine Lord on the altar. This life of dark disappointment was soon interrupted by the arrival in Oldcastle of a Professor of the art of writing in shorthand and of drawing. Among the first pupils who came to him was Mr. Hand. His active mind was ill at ease, so that even the study of this art would be to it a healthy exercise. "Who knows," he said to his mother, as she handed him the fee of a few pounds for the Professor, "but my knowledge "of this branch may be turned into gold for poor "father. I am hopeful, nay, I am confident, that the "Bishop will send me up to Maynooth next year, "and, mother, how happy we should all be if, in "the meantime, I could make some money to help "towards the expenses of my College course."

Passing through Maynooth in those days, was a matter that could not be undertaken with a light heart by one like Mr. Hand. The College was not then under Royal endowment to the same extent as it came to be afterwards. But, did not our Blessed Lord say to His own disciples :— "Consider the ravens, for they sow not, neither do "they reap, neither have they store-house nor barn, "and God feedeth them. How much are you more "valuable than they?" And again :—"Consider "the lilies how they grow : they labour not, neither "do they spin. But I say to you, not even "Solomon in all his glory was clothed like one of "these. Now if God clothe in this manner the "grass that is to-day in the field, and to-morrow is "cast into the oven; how much more you, O ye, "of little faith?"* Mr. Hand was the Lord's chosen disciple, and, therefore, dearer to God than the ravens, " for they sow not, neither do they reap." Surely he must have been far dearer to God than the lilies that " labour not, neither do they spin," and if God cares for them, so that " not even

---

* Luke xii. 24, 27, 28.

"Solomon in all his glory was clothed like one of "them," how much more tenderly will He not now provide what is necessary to bring His chosen disciple into the service of the Sanctuary? And God did so in a manner that God alone could effect.

The Commissariat Department in Maynooth was always an affair of magnitude. At the time of which we are writing, it was administered by only one officer, called the Bursar, but the work was too much for him. In these circumstances, Dr. Montague, the President, resolved to appoint an Assistant, or Under Bursar, to use Father George's expression, who should keep the accounts, and superintend the weighing-out of the daily supplies for the College Dining Hall and Servants' Hall. He was turning over this plan in his mind, and casting about for a fit and proper person to fill the office, when Dr. Cantwell called. The Bishop, from his long experience as College Dean, was in a position to give valuable advice, in reference to the over-worked Department of the Commissariat. Dr. Montague, therefore, very wisely submitted the plan to his distinguished visitor, and the Bishop after approving it, moved by a supernatural impulse, and with the vision of Mr. Hand distinctly before his mind, exclaimed:—" Dr. Montague, you have "created the hour, and I have the man." His Lordship went on to describe Mr. Hand's aptitudes;

to relate the history of his remarkable success and severe trials. "Perhaps," he added with evident emotion, "this fortunate occasion will smooth the "way of a truly deserving young man, to the service "of the altar. Thus, my dear Dr. Montague, you "will be doing an act well-pleasing to God, who "loves Mr. Hand, and the salary attached will ease "his father of what would certainly be to him a "pressing difficulty."

Meanwhile, Mr. Hand had, with wonderful quickness, mastered the art of drawing and writing shorthand, and was actually turning this knowledge into gold, as he had predicted to his mother. The Professor, before many months' tuition, discovered Mr. Hand's extraordinary powers, and appointed him assistant at a small salary, which was religiously laid by for the coming year. One afternoon, when matters were in this state, the postman handed Father George a letter. On opening it he found it to be from the Bishop, who began by expressing his gratification with the wonderful and unexpected working of Divine Providence, which now enabled him to send up Mr. Hand to College. He explained the arrangement with Dr. Montague very fully, and pronounced it to be one of singular advantage. His Lordship concluded with a request that the good news be conveyed, on an early day, to Mr. Hand and his worthy parents. Father George's heart was so full that he had to bury his head in the letter, laying on the table before him, and for some minutes gave vent to his feelings in tears. "How "good is God to my beloved disciple!" he exclaimed ; "do not the angels guard him? The " poor boy is off in Mullingar with the Professor, "turning his knowledge into money to make pro- "vision for next year, but heaven has already "made this provision. How he will exult when "he hears this! 'Behold he cometh, leaping "upon the mountains, skipping over the hills.' I "will rise and go over at once to Stonefield, and "bring sunshine into the gloom there." Musing thus, in the exuberance of his delight, the good priest rose, and looked out from the window of his study in the direction of Stonefield. Strange fancy! He imagined that, in communion with his own feelings, the rays of the warm sun, as far as the eye could reach, were dancing on a golden floor!

It was midsummer, and the landscape had resumed its beauty. The redbreast had gone back to his mates in the thorny thickets, and the swelling notes of countless summer birds were filling the air with their exquisite harmony. *Slieve-na-Cullagh* and *Slieve-Gullion* had put off their white crowns, and were smiling down on the plains below. Again the lowing herds were winding o'er the lea, and the gentle sheep were bleating on the uplands, as Father George left his own door, and walked briskly over to Stonefield. He found the dejected parents within, and, of course, great was their joy at what they heard from him, and deep their gratitude to God. Indeed, it was a visit of sincere and prolonged happiness, for the good priest did not leave until the late evening. A week after this there was more joy in Stonefield when "the beloved disciple," in obedience to a message from Father George, took leave of the Professor at Mullingar, and came home to prepare for College.

Mr. Hand, on entering Maynooth in the August of 1831, encountered the sting of defeat. Most of the men with whom he sat on the same form in the seminary, being intern students, went up to College in the beginning of last session. At their entrance-examination they were weighed and found wanting, and relegated to wander in the mazes of philosophy for another year. They, therefore, considered it a censure, that Mr. Hand now, though a year after them in College, should be allowed to leap on to their bench. It was given out that Dr. Montague had already conceived so profound an esteem for the Assistant Bursar that he registered his name on the roll of the first year's divinity. They felt this and showed their feelings by making ungenerous allusions to Mr. Hand's struggle with poverty, and did not hesitate to characterize the office he had taken to meet the expenses of his College, as an indignity offered to the Diocese of Meath.

This demonstration of a hostile spirit culminated in a conspiracy to disown Mr. Hand, and *scrape* him when he entered the class. Now, *scraping* is the strongest expression of discontent, disapproval, and veiled rebellion on the part of the students in Maynooth, and is happily of rare occurrence. Poor Mr. Hand was, however, subjected to its ignominy, and no one ever more undeservedly. His appearance in the divinity class was greeted with a fierce burst of *scraping* by the malcontents. Startled by the grating noise, he quailed, but in a moment recovered his balance. He quietly took his seat and was soon deep in noting the Professor's lecture, as if he had been all the time breathing freely under a serene sky. The storm thus ushered in by loud thunder claps, lingered in faint echoes for a short time when it died far away from the hallowed walls of the College.

One who witnessed these distressing scenes, assured me that the respect which he entertained for Mr. Hand previously, was now kindled into a reverence that never left him. This gentleman, though of Meath, declined to join in this pitiable exhibition. In giving his lively recollections of this and other events in Mr.

Hand's College career, he stated that while enjoying his constant companionship and confidence, during and after this deplorable episode, he never heard, fall from his lips, one word of complaint against the authors of this wrong. There was no allusion to it whatever, direct or indirect, even in moments of confidential interchange, which brought them often to the very brink of the subject. "Sir," said the friendly informant, "it is not given to many men, down in "this valley of human existence, to witness such a "triumph of Christian forgiveness." And it was this virtue of Christian forgiveness that shone like the sun in Father Hand's life ! No man, professing to follow Chirst, practised this virtue to greater perfection, for no man forgave more cruel rebuffs, more unfounded misrepresentations, and more biting expression of contemptuous looking-down.

We sometimes hear it said that a man is mean-spirited who will not vindicate his honour, who will not insist on his rights. But, surely that cannot be a mean spirit which is a spirit of forgiveness. We must beware of what the world calls a high spirit, for this violates charity. A man hears that his neighbour uttered some calumnies against him. He has not given this neighbour any offence, and he feels, therefore, all the more keenly the sense of the injury done him by this calumny. What is he to do ? He mentions the matter to some intimate friends. The sense of the injury done him fires his blood, and all the others catch the contagion. He has not provoked the calumny; he has always respected his neighbours, and has ever been respected until now. He must not let this pass. What do his friends say? That man has done you an injury; you must not let this calumny pass unnoticed—you owe it to yourself, to your own respectability, to the respectability of your family, of your friends, to repel this calumny. The caluminator must be punished, must be branded. He is in your power; he deserves to feel the weight of your indignation. The injured man is a person of weight in the locality, of large connection, great consideration. He seizes the caluminator, he exposes his crime, holds him up to the execration of the people, perhaps prosecutes him at law, and does everything he can to ruin his credit. His friends say he has acted as became a man of spirit, that he has taught his enemy a lesson, and acted, as he ought, to defend himself. But this time the great Master of all is looking down from His throne of mercy, and He writes in the book of judgment after the name of this man:—"With the same measure you "shall mete withal, it shall be measured to you "again."*

The duty of forgiveness of our neighbour, by

---

* Luke vi. 38.

which we return good for evil, is one inculcated in the Lord's prayer, in which we beg every day and often in the day our Heavenly Father, "to forgive us "our trespasses as we forgive them who trespass "against us." We all love some object, for God has given this faculty to the soul of every human being. By an instinct of nature the parents love their offspring, and the child loves its parents with the warmest affection. The young form attachments; they love ardently friends and companions. Unfortunately they often love the associates of their guilt, and they love not wisely but to destruction. The charity commanded by God is to love unto salvation. St. Paul says :—" Be ye, therefore, " imitators of God, as most dear children, and " walk in love as Christ also hath loved us, and " hath delivered himself up for us, an oblation and " a sacrifice to God for our odour of sweetness." * No doubt we may love our relatives and our friends with a most Christian charity, but if we love any one purely because he ministers to our sinful pleasure; if we love him for his facile approbation of our own evil courses; if our affection for him draws us to approve of his vicious habits, this is a spurious charity, and the reverse of true charity, which must be like that of Christ for us. There is no true charity but that which loves unto salvation.

---

* Epistle to the Ephesians v. 1, 2.

To love those who have been kind to us is, without doubt, an excellent thing; nay, more, the ungrateful soul is odious to God and man. But, the charity for our friends and benefactors is not all that is required in perfect Christian charity. The perfection of Christian charity is that we should love our enemies. Our divine Lord said in His sermon on the Mount:—" You have heard " that it was said, thou shalt love thy neighbour, " and thou shalt hate thy enemy; but I say to you " love your enemies, do good to those that hate " you, and pray for those who persecute you, and " utter calumnies against you; to the end you may " be children of your Father who is in heaven, " who maketh His sun rise upon the good and the " bad, and raineth upon the just and the unjust, " for if you love those that love you, what reward " shall you have ? Do not even the publicans do " this ? " If we are, therefore, to rise to the level of the Christian virtue of charity we must love our enemies, and more than this, we must carry into our outward actions the love of them. We must *do good* to them. If a man say, " I can love my " neighbour who has borne himself in friendly way " towards me, but the man whom I know to be my " enemy I cannot love"—he does not yet know what the Christian virtue of charity is. That man says he finds it impossible to love his enemies! Impossible, let us admit, to pure unregenerate nature.

No doubt the feeling of hatred or revenge may rise in his soul, but has he striven to restrain this feeling as he ought? If he have so striven, the hatred of his enemy will, through God's grace, be conquered like these other spontaneous impulses of the inferior part of the soul, and the man will, amongst the appreciative and higher acts of his soul, elicit the love even of that enemy. This is but the elevation of Christian virtue over merely natural instinct. Clearly, then, the difficulty of loving an enemy, which some might magnify into an impossibility, is, in the merely natural impulses of man, but the human soul, elevated by grace, is capable of this love of an enemy. The same is true of the forgiveness of injuries in our neighbour. The spirit of Christian forgiveness, though somewhat difficult of attainment, may yet be acquired, and through God's grace nourished into an abiding habit in the soul. Even to the Pagan mind the forgiveness of injuries appeared an attribute of heroic greatness. Thus, history admiringly relates of a remarkable Grecian leader, Pericles, that he bore with unbroken patience a fierce attack on his character, which an enemy kept up for the length of a day, and when the night came he lighted a torch and conducted his assailant in safety home! It is set forth as the glory of the great Cæsar that he never forgot a kindness, nor remembered an injury. The most remarkable personages under the Old as well as the New Dispensation, were distinguished by this spirit of forgiveness. Who is not touched by the example of Joseph weeping on the necks of those who had sold him into slavery? Can anything in the history of mankind be more beautiful than the care which King David took that no harm should come to his implacable foe, Saul, who sought his life? But, He in whom every Christian virtue attained its full measure and perfection, has given an example of forgiveness, sufficient to leave the duty a living memory in the minds of all, who know that Jesus Christ came to save them. Prophecy described Him as a lamb led to the slaughter, and that when He was reviled He reviled not again; and if we follow every step of His wonderful life from the night He had to fly into Egypt till he consummated the sacrifice of that life on Calvary, we see the spirit of forgiveness, marking His every relation with men. He held the Universe in the palm of His hand, and yet He bore all kinds of injury without even punishing those who persecuted Him. They attacked Him with the tongue—they heaped up calumnies the most odious against Him—they circulated that He did not regard the law of the Sabbath—that He frequented the worst society—that He was even possessed by the Devil. Then they repeatedly sought to convict Him of some offence against their law. He disarmed them by the gentleness and intelligence of His answers, and when they sought to murder Him, He withdrew privately and hid Himself. In the closing scene of His blessed life, when hanging high upon the tree of the cross, looking down upon those wretched beings, who had nailed Him there, and still filled the air with their shouts of defiance and of hatred; and when He carried His gaze a little further, and looked upon that city, which had Him torn with scourges, crowned with thorns, and covered with spittle, what were His words? "Father, forgive "them, for they know not what they do." Thus, He practised on the Mount beside Jerusalem, what He had taught on the Mount in Galilee :—" Love " your enemies ; do good to them that hate you, and " pray for them that persecute and calumniate you."

It was under the paramount influence of this example of his Divine Master that Mr. Hand prayed for those who wronged him so rudely, so offensively, and so unjustly. He even resolved not to be to them in future the innocent occasion of yielding to that lamentable weakness, which is the worst element in the clay of human nature. With this object he would not strive with them any more in class "for the corruptible crown." During the next three years he sought only "the " incorruptible crown " by scrupulously abstaining from competition with the prizemen, and by designedly but unostentatiously retiring into the humbler ranks of the honour-men. Thus, as he had, in most trying circumstances, copied his divine model in *meekness*, he now copied the same divine model in *humility*. But this action did not meet the approval of Father George. He believed there were circumstances which commanded his beloved disciple "not to put his light in a "hidden place, nor under a bushel: but upon a "candlestick, that they that come may see the "light."* This position Father George represented vigorously and persistently to Mr. Hand every year as the long vacation came round. Against him "the beloved disciple" urged the fact that prizes ought not to engage the attention of one who professed to walk in the footsteps of the Saviour—in fact they took the bloom off the ecclesiastical spirit. Did he not read in the Old Testament that "the prayer of him that humbleth him-"self pierceth the clouds; and he will not depart "till the Most High behold."† ? And in the New "Testament it is written :—" God resisteth the "proud, and giveth His grace to the humble!" ‡ At the same time to get rid of Father George's importunities, and to answer the call of what might be after all an imperative duty, Mr. Hand promised to win for himself a prize in this his fourth or last year. He did so, and Father George tells us all the circumstances :—" When," he says, " Mr.

---

* Luke xi. 33.   † Ecclesiasticus xxxv. 21.   ‡ Ep. St. James iv. 6.

"Hand completed his second year's theology, I
"asked him how it happened he got no premiums?
"'These premiums,' said he, 'I fear do a great
"deal of harm very often. They are a great
"temptation to pride and ambition in after life.'
"I answered, Dr. Doyle and Father Andrew
"Fitzgerald of Carlow, did not think so, though
"Father Staunton, the old President of Carlow, did.
"'Yes,' he replied, 'and Father Staunton was
"right. You know I was proud and ambitious
"when a boy, but sure it is time for me to have
"sense. The books of your circulating library
"have long ago banished a great share of the pride
"of my heart, and it is better for me to have
"nothing to do with these premiums.' But, I
"asked do you see the predicament in which you
"place me? I told Father Power (the President
"of Navan Seminary) you would one day make
"yourself known over the whole world, and I told
"the Bishop you would do the duties of Under-
"Bursar, and obtain premiums with ease. Will
"you do yourself and others an injury and allow
"me to be considered a mere boaster? 'No,'
"said he, 'I never shall. Will you take with the
"sin of it, and I shall obtain a premium?' I will
"with pleasure, I rejoined. 'Very well,' said he,
"'I will obtain some sort of a premium as sure as
"I live.' The year passed, and John Hand, with
"all the duties of Under-Bursar, was called to the

"second premium ! Many who did not know him
"when young thought his talents were only pass-
"able. I do not wonder at this, for St. Ignatius
"never was more anxious to conceal his virtues
"than John Hand was to conceal his talents."

In this truly edifying manner, Mr. Hand accomplished his eventful journey through College. His splendid gifts were veiled behind a charming modesty to disarm envy in others, and at the same time to foster humility in his own heart. But, while scrupulously shunning display, he maintained a fine reputation in his classes all through, and this while under the pressure of grave official duties. His inner life in Maynooth was in its fulness known to God alone : much of it, however, is known to man, and this is enough to make everyone prize his memory and learn a lesson. His mortification of the body and of the spirit, his long watching before Jesus in the Tabernacle—all this, and more is known of him in College. One grand memory he has left behind him in Maynooth, and it was his beautiful practice of doing everything in the most perfect manner. One of the Senior Professors of Maynooth speaking some weeks back of him, said :—" Well, you know Father Hand "was no ordinary priest ; he was an Apostle." Thus the memory of Mr. Hand has descended, and will descend in that great College. Though not of its students, one must feel thankful to reverence it as the mother and nurse of the most devoted ministry in the Church of God. It was here Father Hand received the strong milk which nourished him into the great Apostle to the Catholic exiles from Erin in every strange land. Therefore, it is that All Hallows shall ever continue to greet Maynooth in the words of the Canticle of Canticles:—" My sister, thou art the fountain of " gardens : the well of living waters which run " with a strong stream from Lebanus . . . . .

CHAPTER VI.

A RELIGIOUS AWAKENING.

CONTENTS.—The giving of *Missions* introduced into Ireland by the Priests of St. Vincent of Paul in 1646—Revival of these *Missions* in 1833 by Dean Dowley and a band of young Priests—Mr. Hand hastily withdrew from Maynooth in 1835 to join these Missionaries—He felt that God had destined him for a more arduous work—Rev. Dr. Macnamara—Father Hand engaged in the laborious work of teaching a school—The Nuns devoted to the instruction of poor children—The self-sacrificing life of the Christian Brothers—Father Hand's enormous labours in the Church at Phibsboro'—His powers as a Confessor and a Preacher—His Sermon in Mullingar.

FATHER HAND's dominating principle of never selecting the less perfect of two courses, now determined him to leave College abruptly. Nearly 200 years before this, one of the most effective forces employed by the Catholic Church to secure the salvation of her children was introduced into Ireland. This is the giving of *"Missions"* which St. Vincent of Paul happily inaugurated in this country, at the request of Pope Innocent X., to bring the religious practices of our Catholic people safely through the Red Sea of Cromwell's butcheries. Accordingly, in 1646, St. Vincent chose eight of his followers for this object, and on the eve of their departure thus addressed them:—" Be united and God will bless you; but "let your bond of union be the charity of Christ; "for all other union which is not cemented by "the blood of this Divine Saviour, cannot last. "It is then in Christ, through Christ, and for 'Christ, that you ought to be united, one to "another. The Spirit of Christ is the Spirit of "union and peace. How can you draw souls to "Christ, if you are not united to one another, and "to Himself; go then, as having in Him but one "heart and one intention; and by this means you "will reap some fruit."

The advent of these truly Apostolic men, at the time, was an immense blessing, and though they were able to remain but a few years, and to penetrate into a few places only, they left their track in the vast number of souls brought back to God. It is on record that in these few places, and during these few years they heard 80,000 general confessions. With instructions on the catechism, they combined clear, simple and moving exhortations to the people, to set a high value on their faith, and to keep their lives in harmony with it by a fervent and persistent use of the Sacraments. The local clergy also threw themselves, heart and soul, into the work, and thousands were renouncing sin. The power of the devil had been triumphant, but a new light had now broken in upon his victims. Men saw with a clearness, which made them shudder, that sin had long held sway among them, and that the slavery in which it kept them was of the most degrading character. Sin was a monster whose hideous features they did not know so well before. They did not perceive so plainly the extent of its mischief or the peculiar gravity of its malice. But a prophet had now risen, and the faithful thronged to see and beseech him to cure them.

All the highways leading to these missions brought crowds of pilgrims to the feet of the missionaries, and poured back multitudes into the country, blessing God for the good things that had been done them. Limerick had the principal share in the labours of these holy men, and thither numbers flocked from the countries round, so that the roads to the city were black with people, and this while the Parliamentarian forces in the neighbourhood showed the pilgrims an angry front. The mass of the people was so great in fact, that there was no room in the inns at Limerick. There was not even bread for the thousands that poured into the city. Provisions rose to famine prices, and Limerick was likened to a place taken by storm. The crowd surged about without finding whereon to lay its weary head, and all this was only a repetition of what occurred in the few other centres of these *missions*.

But, the persecution of Catholics which had been gathering outside Limerick, at last rose into a storm, growing more violent every day. The body of the missioners had to fly for their lives, but at the pressing invitation of Dr. O'Dwyer, Bishop of Limerick, three of them remained, and they nobly shared his labours and perils until the memorable siege. How well they did their duty to him and his people in this ordeal is told by the Bishop in a letter to St. Vincent of Paul:—

"I have often in my letters to your Reverence, given you "an account of your missioners in this kingdom: to speak the "truth, never in the memory of man, was so great progress in "the Catholic religion heard of, as we have witnessed within "the last few years, owing to their piety and assiduity. In "the beginning of the present year, we opened the mission "in this city where there are not less than 20,000 communicants; "but, thanks be to God, I doubt not now that many have been "rescued from the jaws of Satan so that drunkenness, cursing, "swearing, and other disorders have been totally abolished, so "that the whole city seems to have changed its face, being com "pelled to have recourse to penance by the war, the famine, the "pestilence, and the dangers which surrounded us on all sides, "and which we receive as manifest signs of the anger of God. "Nevertheless the Divine Goodness has been pleased to do us "this favour, although we are but useless servants; and God has "been pleased to make use of the weak things of this world to "confound the mighty. Even the people of the highest quality "in the city attend so assiduously at the sermons, the "catechetical instructions, and all the other exercises of the "mission, that the Cathedral is scarcely large enough to contain

"all. We know of no better way to appease the anger of God
"than by destroying the sins which are the root and cause of
"all evils. And verily, it is all over with us if God do not
"stretch out to us a helping hand. To Him it belongs to have
"mercy, and to pardon. My good father, I declare to you,
"that to your children I am indebted for the salvation of my
"soul. Write to them some words of consolation. I know
"not, under Heaven, a mission more useful than this of Ireland;
"for although we had a hundred missioners, the harvest of souls
"would be still exceedingly great and the labourers too few."

One of the three missionaries in Limerick had also reported to St. Vincent the condition in which he and his two companions were struggling, and in reply came a message of comfort and consolation, worthy of the great Saint:—

"We have been greatly edified," he wrote, "by your letter,
"seeing in it two excellent effects of the grace of God. By
"the one you have given yourselves to God, to hold on firmly
"in the country, where you are in the midst of perils, choosing
"rather to expose yourselves to death than to be found wanting
"in charity to your neighbour; and by the other you have
"directed your cares to the preservation of your confreres by
"sending them back to France, in order to remove them from
"danger. The spirit of the martyr has inspired you to the
"first, and the virtue of prudence has made you do the second,
"and both the one and the other were drawn from the example
"of our Saviour, who at the point of going to suffer the torments
"of death for the salvation of men, wished to secure and pre-
"serve His disciples, saying: 'Let those go their way, and touch
"them not.' It is thus you have acted as a true child of this
"most adorable Father, to whom I return infinite thanks for
"having produced in you that sovereign charity, which is the
"height of all virtues. I pray Him to fill you with it to the end
"that exercising it in all cases and everywhere, you may pour it
"forth into the breasts of those who want it. Seeing that your

"companions are in the same disposition of remaining, what-
"ever may be the danger from war or pestilence, we are of
"opinion that they should be allowed to stay. How do we
"know what God intends in their regard? Certainly, He does
"not bestow on them so holy a resolution in vain. My God,
"how inscrutable are Thy judgments! Behold at the close of
"one of the most fruitful missions we have ever seen, and,
"perhaps, the most necessary, thou dost stop, as it were, the
"course of Thy mercies upon this penitent city, and dost lay
"Thy hand still more heavily upon her, adding to the misfortune
"of war, the scourge of pestilence. But, all this is done to
"gather in the harvest of the elect, and to collect the good grain
"into Thy eternal granary. We adore Thy ways, O Lord!"

That a whole population could be thus moved to renounce their sinful pleasures, and that not for an occasion, nor for a month, nor a year, but for ever is truly wonderful! No doubt, the scepticism of our day may try to set this fact aside as a fable, written by some enthusiastic admirer. But it is well to remember the words, addressed by the Apostle of the Gentiles to the Corinthians :—"And God is able to make all grace "abound in you: that ye, always having all "sufficiency in all things, may abound to every "good work." *

After a long interval of nearly two hundred years these "*missions*" were revived in Ireland by a band of young priests, who left Maynooth, for this purpose, in the beginning of 1833. These fervent souls were throbbing with earnest suppli-

---

* 2 Corinth. ix. 3.

cation to God for light to know how they could serve Him best, and this light came while the grace of their ordination was fresh upon them. Under its guidance they caught a spark from the sacred fire, kindled by St. Vincent of Paul, and went forth from College to take up again what St. Vincent had been forced by persecution to relinquish nearly two hundred years ago in our unhappy country. The description of this revival in the papers of the day, presents a picture of enthusiasm the like of which has been rarely witnessed. It shows the veneration of our Catholic people for the priests of St. Vincent of Paul, and the breadth and depth of the hold which their *missions* had upon the country. The good they have effected, and continue to effect in the saving of souls, needs no description here. It is a public fact in our midst, in our own time, and under our eyes. We all know it and fully appreciate its extent. So too, we all know the splendid results achieved in this good work by the members of the numerous religious orders and congregations, who in these latter times have been watering what the Fathers of St. Vincent of Paul planted.

The man, who in 1833 started this revival of the *missions* in Ireland, was the late lamented and devoted servant of God, known from the office he held in Maynooth at the time, as Dean Dowley.

In the history of that College no one can be found to have adorned the important office of Dean, as Father Dowley, for no other turned his tenure of that office to the same account for the glory of God. Of him it may be truly said that the zeal for saving souls burned in his heart as the oil is consumed in the lamp! Now, since good priests are the great factor in saving souls, he literally spent himself in making the students, who passed through his hands in College, good priests. It is no vain boast to say that Irish Catholics had always zealous pastors, and to this blessing they owe that attachment to their religion, for which they are so distinguished. Dean Dowley took care to foster the true ecclesiastical spirit among the students under his charge, by a system of private unions for purposes of prayer, in which he was himself the first to join. And in 1826 when the members of the Royal Commission, appointed to report on the general state of education in Ireland, attempted profanely to bring these private practices of devotion in Maynooth into their field of inquiry, Dean Dowley repelled their presumption in forcible and spirited terms. In reply to the question of the peculiar advantages or inducements belonging to the pious unions in which these private devotions are carried on, he said:—" As members " of this pious Confraternity, they have no induce- " ments, or advantages but such as are entirely and "exclusively spiritual and religious. Here, with "sentiments of great respect for this Board, I beg "leave to submit whether subjects purely and "strictly religious, practices merely of Catholic "discipline adopted in the College, are legitimate "matters of investigation. The authority of the "visitors of the College is restricted by Act of "Parliament, and does not extend to points, which "belong exclusively to the doctrine or discipline "of the Roman Catholic religion. Whether the "powers of this Commission are more extensive, "it is not for me to determine." It is hardly necessary to add that the Dean was asked no more questions on this subject.

Dean Dowley's burning zeal for saving souls was not satisfied with the training of good pastors. Though he had a keen relish for the intellectual luxuries of Maynooth, and a singular aptitude for his official duties there, yet he was not happy. He reflected on the many earnest priests he sent forth, and that while intellectually they may be his inferiors, they were giants compared to him in gathering in the harvest of Jesus Christ. "What," he used to say, "men without letters rise up and "take heaven by violence, and I, with all my "learning, have hardly put in my sickle though "the harvest is come." In fits of great mental agony over this reflection his thoughts were after the manner of those set forth in the New

Testament, where they may be read in the Gospel of St. John iv., 35, 36, in these suggestive words of our Blessed Lord to His disciples :—" Do not you say, there are yet four "months and then the harvest cometh? Behold "I say to you, lift up your eyes, and see the "countries, for they are white already to harvest. "And he that reapeth receiveth wages, and "gathereth fruit unto life everlasting." From all this it is easy to see how Dean Dowley became the centre of a circle of fervent students, who, during their last year in College, were striving to form a plan for reviving the missions of St. Vincent of Paul in Ireland. In their secret deliberations they were met at every step by formidable difficulties which were springing under their feet. At last Dean Dowley impatient of their delay, one day after their admission to priests' orders, quickened them into immediate action by words to this effect:—"Why stand here all the day "idle? go at once into the vineyard, and the "Lord of the vineyard will reward your generous "sacrifice by maturing your rule and plan of "life in His own good time," and immediately they departed from Maynooth. The Dean followed some time after, and they adopted the rule of St. Vincent of Paul under the name of "The "Fathers of the Congregation of the Mission," who from that day have grown here in usefulness, and to be "the good odour of Christ "unto God."

This company of fervent priests directly on retiring from Maynooth, took a house on Usher's Quay, and with the sanction of Dr. Murray, the venerated Archbishop of Dublin, they opened a day school there, in addition to their special work of giving *Missions* through the country, which they were not able to begin for some time later on. They fixed their residence in Dublin in 1833, and in due course Castleknock, with its fine demesne, on the border of the Phœnix Park, fell into their hands. This was an important acquisition, because the training of youth for the Sanctuary is a part of the rule of the Fathers of the Congregation of the Mission, and Castleknock enabled them at once to open a diocesan seminary, a proposal which was readily accepted by the pious Archbishop Murray. But dearer still to the priests of St. Vincent of Paul is that part of their rule which directs them to have a church among the poor, as a training school for their missionaries. In this matter, provision, though not immediate, was not far distant, for His Grace Dr Murray had already engaged to place Dean Dowley and his zealous companions, in charge of the poorest and most laborious mission on the suburbs of the city.

In the meantime Mr. Hand in Maynooth conceived an ardent admiration for the Fathers of

the Congregation of the Mission, and in order to join in their holy work, he, though called to priests' orders, severed his connection with the diocese of Meath. In writing to his father of this resolve, and in bidding him a tender farewell, he added that from the time he felt himself invited into the Sacred Ministry, his mind was never to enrich his friends. He thanked God that his life now would preclude the possibility of his making money, even if he were so inclined. After this he withdrew hastily from the College in June, 1835, and went straight to Castleknock. The circle there was gladdened by the accession of this devout, kindred spirit, and they loved him the more, when sometime afterwards he declared, with tears in his eyes, that while immensely comforted in being associated with them, he shrunk from entering their noviciate or taking their vows. A voice from heaven bade him wait—God had destined him for a still more arduous and painful mission! Rev. Dr. Macnamara, one of that circle, and at present the learned Rector of the Irish College at Paris, has been kind enough to describe the effect of Mr. Hand's action on this occasion:—" Father Hand," to use Dr. Macnamara's words, " contracted no community obliga-
" tions with us, and was quite free, as far as we
" were concerned, to devote himself to any other
" course of life. Nevertheless he continued to his

"dying hour to entertain towards us the deepest
"esteem and the most earnest affection, as we on
"our part followed him with our best wishes, into
"the destination which the Almighty God reserved
"for him, and our feelings ripened into admiration
"for him, as we witnessed how marvellously God
"had blessed his work."

Mr. Hand was ordained priest on the 13th December, 1835, in the private chapel of St. Vincent's Seminary at Castleknock, by the Right Rev. Dr. Clancy, Vicar Apostolic of British Guiana. He was not bound by the vows of his companions, and yet there was not one among them shared their apostolic labours in Dublin with a more burning zeal. This is very beautifully and very generously expressed by the Rev. Dr. Macnamara when he says:—" Father Hand had
"his share in all this work, and I fondly recall his
"unreserved devotion to the various services so
"long as he remained. I retain even after so long
"a lapse of time a vivid recollection of the
"edification he gave us by his personal piety and
"fervent observance of all the forms of com-
"munity life."

Father Hand received the baptism of his labours as a teacher in the Day School on Usher's Quay, where Dean Dowley sent him to assist. To his work here he brought prodigious vigor of mind and body, and it was taxed to the very fullest extent. Any one even slightly acquainted with the life of a teacher in a crowded school, must realize that its drudgery, and its tedious monotony are enough to tax the patience and fervour of an Apostle. And yet people do not properly estimate the laboriousness of the work of teaching, especially in the schools of the poor. The student who spends but eight hours a day at a study, which requires a vigorous application of his mental faculties to the subject, is pale and emaciated. Now, the work of the school-teacher demands an application of the mind, more constant and more intense than any ordinary study. If the heart of a hard student would fail him at the prospect of six or eight hours of mental effort at a stretch, though animated by fond ambition or the pleasing conviction that he is adding to his stock of learning, how should he regard the strain on his faculties for ten or twelve hours continuously without any such stimulus to sustain him? Then, how should he feel if he were, during these ten or twelve long hours, obliged to be in a cheerless and comfortless room? How should he feel if he were under the necessity of living not only in such a room every day for seven or eight hours, but being all this time hemmed in by a crowd of poor boys or girls, inhaling an air, laden with the reekings of clothes, saturated with rain, or the foul breath of a badly nourished and unwashed multitude? This is not intended as a sneer at the poor. Now, such is the daily life of thousands amongst us. We must, therefore, accord our sympathy to that indispensable body of good Irishmen and Irish women, who are engaged in this laborious profession of teaching.

This feeling of sympathy is heightened into one of profound admiration when it is directed to those noble souls who, for love of Jesus Christ, have condemned themselves to the work of instructing the children of the poor in the midst of surroundings, not unlike what Milton spoke of when he said:—

> "There I, a prisoner chained, scarce freely draw
> The air imprisoned also, close and damp,
> Unwholesome draught."

They are those gentle ladies who sweeten the sinful atmosphere of all our large cities and towns with the example of their pure and holy lives.

That such innocence, loveliness, and gentle breeding should, without earthly reward, consecrate highly-cultivated minds to the severe mental strain of many hours daily in teaching poor children, covered with rags and filth, and in the unwholesome atmosphere described, is a matter to command not merely our sympathy, but our reverence.

But this esteem and reverence are due in fuller measure and higher degree, to those devoted men, who offer to their Divine Master, the sacrifice of their lives for the instruction of poor boys, and seal this sacrifice by a solemn vow to labour till death in this painful task without ever venturing to aspire to a higher calling. Who can stand on the grave of Gerald Griffin and not feel within him an admiration, kindled with enthusiasm, for the self-sacrificing life of a Christian Brother? And a greener or more unpretending grave it is not easy to see. Every person who goes to Cork ought to pay it a visit, and as one strays through the sacred nook, under the shadows of the varied trees, he will learn an important lesson. He cannot fail also to carry away with him the reflection, that it is no wonder one, who gave such brilliant talents, and gilded prospects to the humble but meritorious occupation of a Christian Brother, should desire to sleep his "sleep that knows no "waking" within the shadow of the place where he sealed his labours with death. And God has marked His value of this life of sacrifice of the Christian Brothers by the results with which He has blessed their work in this country. In 1804, they began with but one school, and to-day we have the splendid result of 40,000 boys, being taught by the Christian Brothers not only secular learning, but that knowledge which will enable those boys to encounter the enemies of their eternal salvation.

Father Hand spent many hours a-day for nearly two years in the day school on Usher's Quay. In the year 1838 Archbishop Murray handed over to Dean Dowley and his devout community the Church at Phibsboro', with its extensive and populous neighbourhood. Phibsboro' was then a most unpromising suburb, and it seems to have been a moral desert as far as religion was concerned:—"On going there," says Dr. Macnamara, "we found ourselves in face of an "apostolic work, the reformation of a people, who "had acquired an unenviable notoriety by the "disorders of every kind fearfully prevalent in the "locality all round. The population was made up "of the outlying inhabitants of four different "parishes, who being so remote from their paro-"chial churches, were, therefore, very much as "sheep without a pastor. We accordingly applied "ourselves to the work as we found it, feeling that "'a wide and manifest door' was opened to us "for whatever zeal we could bring to what we "regarded a divinely appointed mission. Our "preaching was 'in season and out of season,' and "we devoted long hours to the confessional, "whether penitents came or not. For a time, "indeed, we had leisure not only for our office in "the holy tribunal, but for the study of theology "besides. But, as a few weeks passed on, we "were so besieged, that hearing confessions should "be to us a day and night-work, did we not limit "our time by a rigid adherence to the observance "of hours. We had the happiness of seeing the "results through God's blessing 'in a renewal of "'the face of the earth,' so that Phibsboro' by its "work became in the order of God's providence, "a normal school for our missions in due course of "time." Such is the picture of Phibsboro' at that period, and such was the vineyard for which Father Hand volunteered in the third year of his ministry.

It is not easy for the young of the present generation to realize the church at Phibsboro' so late as fifty years ago. The priests of the congregation of the Mission, with Father Hand, counted but few in number. Their church was a small dark chamber, and their dwelling a miserable shed at one end of the most wretched part of the city. In this new field Father Hand became a more active, and certainly a more distinguished labourer than in that which he had left. He seems to have discovered new powers in himself, and the work he did was immense. Though of a tender frame, for he had in him the germs of consumption, he was at work at four o'clock in the morning, and did not go to bed early. He spent many hours a day in the confessional, and this duty is one of the most anxious and responsible that a priest has to transact. Go into a church; you see him in a small box. There is not even the interest of recognition, and yet the attention must never flag. Cases involving many complications in the matter of restitution, of charity, of duty are constantly put before the confessor, and he must generally decide at once. In all this there is the severest strain on the mind of the confessor, while his body is exposed often to the chill or damp of the church. Father Hand gave the best part of his days to hearing confessions, especially of the poor. His marvellous power of comforting the despondent in the Sacred tribunal may be gathered from a touching incident related of him. There was in Dublin just then a wealthy and popular Catholic gentleman, who adored his young wife for the qualities of head and heart with which God had endowed her. They were blessed with one son and one daughter, who possessed all that makes youth and beauty lovable. Such was the family circle, and the light of their happy home was as the light that fills the summer sky, when it was put out with terrible suddenness. Death unexpectedly summoned the good father, who was soon followed by his two beloved children. A dark shadow had fallen on the mother's heart —it was the shadow of despondency. She sought consolation from her confessor, and in vain did he try to heal her aching heart by the solemn charge to remember that "there is a hope, there is a joy, which this faithless world can never destroy."

Weighed down and broken with a great sorrow, she took the veil in a community of Nuns, devoted to the care of the worst-afflicted among God's creatures. Still she was not able to forget the affliction which Heaven had sent. It kept haunting her as in a ghastly dream, until Father Hand banished it for ever. He often came to the Convent on his mission of charity, and one evening she told him after confession her sad story and how its awful vision kept constantly flitting before her disconsolate spirit. He listened so far into the darkness that he could see nothing, but heard the moaning of the broken and despondent heart. At length he ventured to address to her words, such as those of the Prophet:—" For the affliction " of the daughter of my people I am afflicted and " made sorrowful, astonishment hath taken hold on " me. Is there no balm in Gilead? or is there no " physician there? Why then is not the wound " of the daughter of my people closed?" * Thus he went on speaking words of comfort until she felt her heart melting into a joy which it had not known for many years. She rose quite elated from her knees, and often afterwards mentioned the incident in proof of her conviction that he who was able to expel this deep sorrow which darkened her soul for so long a period, must have been a great servant of God.

* Jeremias viii. 21, 22.

Father Hand preached often, and as a preacher he was also successful. His voice was not strong, but it was as the sound of the silver bell. He did not speak with the stiffness of a book, nor the common place of careless conversation. The style he adopted was easy and dignified, such as went direct to the hearts of his audience. His wonderful earnestness, or, as one who often listened to him expressed it, "his pounding away," his impressive manner, his truthful modest face, gave him complete control over those who came to hear him. He was now in the freshness of a man of 32, and was remarked for the benevolent expression of his countenance. He was above the middle height, but not commanding in stature, for he allowed his head and shoulders to droop. His carriage and address were those of a holy priest. Therefore his silvery voice, his truthful modest face, his wonderful earnestness of manner, and unaffected simplicity of language, could not but make his discourse effective.

It would appear that in preparing to preach the book he studied was the Bible. Dr. M‘Elroy stated a most interesting fact to show this, which was, perhaps, the best element in the success of Father Hand's career. "I was curate," said Dr. M‘Elroy, "at Mullingar in 1846, and "living in the bishop's house. Early in the spring "of that year I remember Father Hand coming to

" my room on the evening of a Saturday. He ap-
" peared cold and hungry, after having driven over
" a long and tiring country in quest of alms for
" All Hallows, and yet he would have nothing
" but the evening tea to which the bishop had in-
" vited him on hearing of his arrival. We chatted
" on in the drawing-room until I had to go out on
" some parochial duty. Before leaving, however,
" the bishop, at my suggestion, asked Father
" Hand to preach at the last Mass next day. I
" then left, and Father Hand, coming away in a
" few minutes after, begged me to fetch a New
" Testament to his room that he might get some
" ideas for his sermon. I did so, and in handing
" him the book I said there was a large supply of
" published sermons in my little library, and he
" could have any he wished. While I was thus
" speaking he glanced at the gospel for the Sunday,
" and then raising his eyes towards me he quietly
" said :—' Don't take any further trouble ; I shall
" have matter enough here.' Accordingly he
" preached the following day, and I had to attend
" a distant sick-call. But returning late in the
" afternoon I found the bishop loud in praise of
" Father Hand's sermon, and during the following
" week the town was literally ringing with admira-
" tion for the preacher. I assure you that seven
" years after the event I heard that sermon talked
" of with the most retentive memory by the people

"of Mullingar, and yet the only book Father Hand
"studied for it was the copy of the New Testa-
"ment that I gave him. To you, no doubt, this
"is a beautiful fact. but to me it is a sad memory,
"for it was the last occasion I saw my dear friend,
"Father Hand, alive."

Father Hand possessed a marvellous facility of preaching, and this may have been due to his earnest and exclusive study of the Scriptures. His sister, Mrs. Tanham, remembers hearing him preach three sermons in the church at Kells one St. Patrick's Day, and apparently without an effort, though in the intervals he had his hands filled with other anxious occupation. True, his sermons were peculiarly his own. Apparently without an effort, and very simple, while they moved everyone who heard them.

The Apostles "were filled with the Holy Ghost,
"and they began to speak with divers tongues
" . . . . so that the devout men of every
"nation under heaven . . . . wondered say-
"ing . . . . how have we heard, every man
"our own tongue wherein we were born ? . . .
"Strangers of Rome, Jews also, and proselytes,
"Cretes and Arabians : we have heard them
"speak in our own tongues the wonderful works
"of God." *

It is a saying of the great Cardinal Bellarmin,

---

* Acts of the Apostles, ii. 4-11.

that the Apostles could speak Greek, but not more fluently than Demosthenes; they could speak Latin, but not more elegantly than Marcus Tullius. For the means ought to be proportioned to the end, which was to inculcate the faith and the law of God, not by a profuse display of words, and dignity of speech, but by the power of the Spirit. Father Hand spoke as if a tongue of fire had descended on him. Now, there is a tongue for the hardened sinner—a tongue of fire—and with this tongue he moved the hard hearts. There is a tongue for the "wolf," and the "thief"—a tongue rushing like a strong wind, and with this tongue he more than once forced back "the destroyer." There is a tongue for the Christian soldier—a comforting tongue—and with this he kindled the ardour and the hopes of hesitating souls. There is a tongue for the weak, and a tongue for the strong, a tongue for the old, and a tongue for the young, a tongue for the educated man of the world, and a tongue for the unlettered sons of toil, and all these tongues Father Hand knew. There is yet another tongue, a tongue for the widow and the orphan—a tender sympathetic tongue, and this tongue he knew best of all. Thus the gift of tongues was given to Father Hand, and so it was that " the strangers " from Rome, Jews also, and proselytes, Cretes and " Arabians heard him speak in their own tongues " the wonderful works of God."

When St. Paul wrote to Timothy charging him "to preach the word, to be instant in season and "out of season," he warned him at the same time that "the servant of God must not wrangle, but be "mild towards all men." These words of the Apostle point out the special charm of Father Hand's discourses. He preached the Word; he exhorted "in season and out of season," but he did not wrangle; he was mild towards all men. Mildness seemed the very essence of his nature. For those who have had so many evidences of his disposition in this respect, it were quite superfluous to adduce illustrations which might be multiplied. War, it cannot be denied, is a great force, but peace is a much greater. The storm sweeps noxious vapours from the heavens, and stirs the stagnant waters, but it is the serene season of peace gives to victory its blossoms, and its fruit. Peace was the power to which Father Hand most trusted, and we have in the traditions of All Hallows very striking memorials of the telling effect with which he used it in never making an enemy.

Father Hand also said Mass every morning, and keen, indeed, was his love for the Holy Sacrifice, even when it was not a duty but a devotion. It has been mentioned in connection with this, that in the throes of his last illness he had an altar fitted up in his sick room, and offered up the Holy

Sacrifice on it for two consecutive days, but in attempting this the third day, he fell back exhausted. From this moment his slender strength declined until it departed for ever.

CHAPTER VII.

AN INSPIRATION.

CONTENTS.—Father Hand's inspiration to establish a College for the education of Missionaries to minister to Irish Catholics abroad—His plan of carrying out this project—He is pronounced rash by those from whom he expected encouragement—His earnest confidence won the support of Archbishop Murray—He is sent to the National Board Normal School, Marlborought Sreet, to give religious instruction to the Teachers in Training—A distinguished writer is deeply impressed by his method of teaching the Catechism—His interview with Archbishop Murray—His letter to every Bishop in Ireland on his proposed College.

ABOUT the year 1838, the Rev. Mr. O'Toole, a learned and earnest Irish priest, who had been educated on the Continent, arrived in this country from France. He was instructed with the mission of recommending to the Catholics of Ireland, the *Association for the Propagation of the Faith*, and Dr. Murray, the Archbishop of Dublin, gave him a most cordial reception. The work of the Association soon prospered, and among the first to establish a branch of it were the Fathers of the Congregation of the Mission, in their little church at Phibsborough. Father Hand took charge of this, for time was developing in him day by day new springs of action, and the years as they rolled on were extending the field of his marvellous zeal. The Annals of the Association kindled all the enthusiasm of his nature, and as he often read them far into the night, the martyrs, who left a crimson-stain on many a heathen land in the East, passed before him, wearing their crowns and waving their palms. Turning to the perilous wanderings of the missionaries in the great *lone land* of the West, he thought of the scattered children of his own race and creed. He saw them by the mighty rivers of America, like the Jews in their captivity, who "sat upon the rivers of Babylon, and wept when they remembered Sion." He followed them into the regions of the Southern Cross, into the bush, into the mine, and he found them begging the bread of life, but no missionary to break it to them. His thoughts travelled back near home, and among the population that throng England's and Scotland's great cities, thousands of poor Irish Catholics were heard calling for an Irish priest. One night he went to bed so excited by this reflection that it disturbed his much-needed rest. He dreamt of the poor Catholic exiles from Ireland, and their cry of spiritual distress was startling in his sleep. It seemed to convey to him a message from God to send them missionaries, and he resolved to do so.

Father Hand believed firmly that the spiritual

wants of a people, are, as a rule best cared by priests who are racy of the soil of the people to whom they minister. Therefore, he prayed earnestly for light and aid to enter upon his commission from above by sending forth missionaries who are themselves Irishmen. Every morning at the altar, and, during the day, prostrate for hours in presence of the Blessed Sacrament, he poured forth his petitions to God until the light and the aid came. Under their influence he noted the superabundant graces of Apostolic vocation possessed by our Catholic youth. The ardour with which these vessels of election desired "to go out "from their country and their people to the land "which the Lord would show them," made a deep impression upon him, and he determined to open a field where they might revive the ancient glories of this Island of Saints, and shed benediction on its exiled race. The proper material was thus pointed out to him at hand, but how was this material to be moulded? By establishing, near Dublin, a College for the Foreign Missions; and he felt sure his Catholic fellow-countrymen would generously give him the means of building and supporting such an institution. The people, who, in every age, sustained the missionary in his pilgrimage, and who, at the present moment, were contributing in liberal measure to the funds of the Association for the Propagation of the Faith,

would, he was assured, be true to the traditional destiny of Ireland, and give, even of their slender means, to send missionaries to save the souls of their perishing countrymen. "It was," says Dr. Macnamara, "at Phibsboro' Father Hand con-
"ceived the idea of a College for Foreign
"Missions. It was inspired by the Association
"for the Propagation of the Faith, which just at
"that period was introduced into Ireland. We
"almost at once instituted a branch of the Associ-
"ation at Phibsboro', and Father Hand, by the
"share he had in the good work, and witnessing the
"zeal and generosity of the faithful for its promo-
"tion, caught up the idea that a College for the
"Foreign Missions would be sure of success."

Father Hand's heart was so full of gratitude to heaven for this light and aid, that again and again he expressed his thanksgiving in the most fervent manner. All the resources of his mind were immediately laid under contribution in drawing up a plan to give practical effect to his inspirations. This document, though hastily put together, shows the extent to which he had been favoured, from the very start, with the whisper- ings of divine grace. In it the number of students he proposes to begin with is fixed at 200, and the expenses of their collegiate training he sets down at £6,000 a year. "Let the number of "students," he says, "in the College be 200—

"more, perhaps, than can be expected to be
"received for a few years. Now, £25 a year
"allowed for each student, would, if managed with
"economy, cover all expenses, when the 200 are
"living in common and supplied with good whole-
"some food, and 200 students at £25 each in the
"year, would be £5,000.

"The support of the superiors and professors
"will not be overrated if set down at £600 a year,
"for I have no difficulty in saying that persons
"capable of filling these situations could be found
"who would be satisfied with food and raiment,
"and without fixed salaries. The president and
"vice-president would also profess some classes,
"and thus lessen the expenditure. Now this
"£600 added to £5,000 will make £5,600, and
"allowing £400 a year for contingent expenses,
"attendant on the College, we shall have in all
"£6,000, the annual expenditure of the College
"for 200 students." This sum he firmly believes
will be permanently supplied in a few years from
the interest on accumulated donations and be-
quests, but in the meantime it must be raised by
begging from door to door, and in words that
breathe the most beautiful spirit of self-sacrifice he
offers his own services for this purpose. "I will,"
he says, "most freely devote my time and facul-
"ties gratuitously to this holy work, should God
"by means of my ecclesiastical superiors choose

"to make use of my poor and unworthy labours in "that way."

"Again I say every year would be more than "able to stand for itself, for every year is sure to "bring in as much as will defray all the expenses "of the College for that year. Then, I am almost "certain that the College would·in a few years "have funds to a very considerable extent, arising "either from charitable donations, legacies or be-"quests, made by the faithful, both clergy and "laity, to found burses. The charity is one most "likely to engage the favour of the pious and "zealous, so that I think before ten years shall "have elapsed the College, if founded now, will "stand in need of very little in the form of *yearly* "*contributions.*

"But let us suppose that no money were to "remain on hands after the first year, and that "no foundations would be made for the education "of young priests for the Foreign Missions till "after some years to come. This is only a sup-"position, for the contrary will assuredly be the "fact; but let it be admitted for a moment, and "even on this assumption, I say that the College "would and could be maintained by *yearly con-*"*tributions.* Thus adapting a very moderate "standard, I may calculate upon each bishop in "Ireland contributing annually the sum of £5, "that is a total of £135; each parish priest £2

"annually, that is £2,000; each curate £1 annu-
"ally, that is £2,000; each parish £5 annually,
"that is £5,145; and wealthy individuals of zeal
"every year collectively £2,000. Total, £11,270.

"Now half this sum would almost suffice for
"the expenses of the College, and I have no diffi-
"culty in saying that, with the assistance of God,
"there will be money enough for the support of
"200 or 300 students with their superiors and
"professors."

Having thus sketched the broad lines on which he hoped to meet the annual expenditure of his proposed Foreign Missionary College, he proceeds to indicate how to provide for purchasing the proper plant, and defraying the other expenses of beginning the work. A suitable building with the necessary furniture, and surrounded by ample grounds, could, he thinks, be secured for about £12,000, and this sum he pledges himself in the fulness of his zeal to collect from the laity in less than six months:—"This sum" (£12,000), he says, "I would pledge myself to collect among the
"lay portion of the faithful in less than six months.
"I undertake to do so with the leave and counten-
"ance of the bishops and clergy of Ireland, and
"above all aided by Almighty God, who knows
"how to make use of the weakest instruments to
"accomplish great things."

Then, for whatever would be necessary to defray

the other expenses of opening the institution, he relies upon the support of the bishops and priests of Ireland in their respective localities, but chiefly on the funds at the disposal of the Association for the Propagation of the Faith, "since," to quote his words, "*£20 expended on the education here in Ireland of a young priest for the Foreign Missions, would go further to propagate the Faith than £100 sent off to distant missions.*"

These interesting views he proposes as follows :
—" Let it now be supposed that the bishops of
" Ireland, who are to be the patrons and guardians
" of the College, recommend this truly charitable
" and great work to the zeal of their priests, and
" that the priests would propose and recommend it
" to the charity of the faithful in their respective
" parishes. It is not too much to expect that, on an
" average, each parish should bring in £10—that
" is, £10 from 1,029 parishes or £10,290, inde-
" pendent of the donations of the priests them-
" selves.

" The charity of wealthy individuals of piety
" and zeal may be calculated upon as likely to
" realize at least £2,000 or £3,000. Many wish-
" ing at their death to bequeath part of their pro-
" perty to charitable purposes, will very probably
" consider the said College.

" The Association for the Propagation of the
" Faith will, if such an allocation be not contrary

"to the spirit of their Institution, give a couple of "thousand pounds. Twenty pounds expended on "the education here in Ireland of a young priest "for the Foreign Mission would go further to "propagate the Faith than £100 sent off to distant "nations. Therefore, I think, the Association "without in any way departing from its spirit, "could and would assist our College for the "Foreign Missions."

Coming now to that stage when the College is actually established, he gives his views in a general way, as to the government and discipline which ought to control it. After placing the Institution under the patronage of the bishops of Ireland, he adds:—

"Nothing shall be left undone to secure the "services of pious, learned and experienced "Superiors and Professors, whose example as "well as word may edify and instruct the "students, so as to form them to virtue, and "give in one word tone and temper to the "College.

"The Superiors and Professors shall dine, "&c., with the Students in the same Refectory and "at the same hours. Not only the regular dis-"cipline of the College, but the welfare of the "Students, and their efficiency afterwards on the "Missions, will depend in a great measure on "this.

"The Professors shall contribute to the advancement of learning and piety among the Students by taking recreation with them as often as possible, by joining them on the public walks, and by making them feel that it is good and pleasant for brothers to live together.

"From the governing body a Council shall be selected and entrusted with the management of the College. It shall be the bounden duty of this Council to maintain in full force and at all times, the rules and discipline. They shall have charge of examining all candidates for admission to the College, with full power to exclude any whom they may consider ineligible, no matter by whom recommended. Every means that prudence and charity may suggest shall be employed by them to find out by inquiry from persons in the country or otherwise, whether or not the candidates presenting themselves are properly qualified for the sublime calling and arduous undertaking to which they aspire, in offering themselves to the work of the Foreign Missions.

"No candidate shall be received into the College unless he have the intention of taking holy orders, and of devoting himself to the Foreign Missions. He shall also be qualified to enter the Logic class, and hence a part of the Vacations, as well as a few hours every week, "ought to be set apart for Latin and Greek "studies, to afford those who may need it an "opportunity of being sufficiently prepared in "these languages. But there shall be no special "Humanity or Rhetoric class in the College.

"Having passed his entrance examination, the "candidate shall enter on a spiritual retreat of "eight or ten days, with the object of making a "general confession, and consulting God still "further as to his vocation. The Superiors shall "on their part, during that time, endeavour by "prayer and otherwise to discover his qualifica- "tions and disqualifications, in order that at the "end of his retreat they may determine on re- "ceiving or rejecting him.

"As piety is equally, even more, necessary "for a priest than learning, the student's time "shall be so divided as to leave a sufficient "margin for the cultivation of piety and learning, "both being absolutely necessary for a good "priest."

This purpose filled Father Hand's imagination, and kept rising until it grew into a feeling of the keenest distress. "The conception," writes Dr. Macnamara, "cast him into a great embarrass- "ment between the impulse by which he felt "himself urged to embark in the undertaking on "the one side, and the vastness of the project on "the other." To obtain relief he laid bare the

workings of his mind to those who, he believed, would guide him, but they received his confidence with a cold reserve. They expressed misgivings; they raised difficulties; and in the end told him plainly that his project seemed like an attempt to quarry the granite-rock with a razor, or moor the great ship with a thread of silk. But these chilling dissuasions Father Hand confronted with a courage which won the powerful support of the Venerated Archbishop Murray. This is well told by Dr. Macnamara, when he says:—" He
" was young, had no position, possessed no in-
" fluence of any kind, and was unknown outside
" the community and the congregation, attending
" what was then the little church of Phibsborough.
" He was so humble and modest that he felt the
" greatest difficulty in revealing his design to any
" one, and so far as he took courage to do so,
" objections of all sorts were pressed upon him.
" These objections he felt unable to answer, except
" by saying he could not resist the urgency he felt
" within him to engage in the enterprise. In fact
" he felt himself called, as he could not help
" believing, by a call from heaven, to undertake
" a work which he could scarcely see how even to
" set about. However, amidst the objections he
" had to encounter on all sides, he was favoured
" with one voice of encouragement. It came from
" the Venerable Archbishop, Most Rev. Dr.

"Murray, who during his long and prosperous
"Episcopate, saw so many institutions spring up
"around him, beginning with humble commence-
"ments, and carried out by agencies so dispropor-
"tionate, humanly speaking, with the results
"arrived at. Encouragement from such a source
"Father Hand regarded as oracular, and he ac-
"cordingly committed himself to his project as
"a mission divinely appointed for him."

Dr. Murray is mentioned in one of the literary publications of his time as :—"A Bishop who has
"few equals throughout Christendom. In his
"own country he stands unrivalled. Some men
"have faculties lofty, yet rugged and uneven, like
"the towering Alps. They have passions which
"when evoked put us in mind of the ocean, lashed
"by a tempest. They are bright suns that on
"close examination display many spots. They
"are like diamonds with the front polished—the
"sides dim. Far different, though not less re-
"markable, is the character of Archbishop Murray.
"He possesses preeminence with perfect even-
"ness of mind. He has determination of soul
"equal to the greatest occasions. He is a bright
"sun standing the test of the closest scrutiny, and
"advancing with increased splendour." And, without doubt, Dr. Murray's Episcopate was as "a
"spring that bubbleth fast and gave out saving
"waters in great abundance." Indeed, it can be

truly said of him that he found the church of Dublin thrust into the cold shade, and he brought it out into the warm light. His patriotism may be criticised unfavourably by the politician of the present day, but if the life of Dr. Murray as a citizen be regarded, he had certainly the good of the whole community at heart, and hence the whole community honour his memory. In Dublin there are many out of every class who, in our Catholic Cathedral, do reverence before that cold marble, which as they pass by, brings back to their memories the familiar features of the great churchman.

At this stage in Father Hand's career, he is to be seen in the National Board Normal School, Marlboro' Street, giving religious instruction to the teachers in training, a work which was soon after forbidden, and is still prohibited by his Ecclesiastical Superiors. To understand this apparently awkward circumstance, it will be necessary to go back to the year 1831, when the system of Irish National Education passed into law. Archbishop Murray was convinced that to exclude religion from all secular education is opposed to one of the most fundamental of Catholic principles. He held that to teach a boy mathematics, and other secular branches, without teaching him at the same time to respect his parents, not to steal, nor to lie, is a bad education, and calculated to breed mischief to the state not less than the individual. This boy may go on adding daily to his stock of secular knowledge; he can learn a vast variety of what takes place upon the earth, and under the earth, but all this does not lead him one step towards his everlasting happiness. Therefore, the "one thing necessary" in the education of our youth is to teach them to avoid vice, practise virtue, and by a knowledge of their holy religion to prepare them to enter upon life where the waves of human passion roll highest. That it was in this way Dr. Murray thought, there can be no doubt. Hence the measure of Irish National Education, granted by the State in 1831, he did not regard as abstractedly the best, but incomparably better than the primary schools then existing, and the best that could be obtained in the circumstances. Upon these grounds of expediency, he and most of the Irish Bishops accepted the system of National Education, when it started on the principle of "combined literary, and separate religious education," and that they acted on sound principles, would appear from instructions, sought and obtained from Rome at the time.

In 1839, some of the Irish Bishops submitted to the Holy See, the following query :—" Can the "system of National Education in Ireland, having "regard to its nature and form, be so tolerated that "Catholics may avail themselves of it?" This was referred to by Pope Gregory XVI., to the Sacred Congregation *De Propaganda Fide*, who became greatly exercised over it. At last after a long, and anxious consideration the members, at their meeting of the 22nd December, 1840, drew up a body of instructions, which were approved by the Sovereign Pontiff, and forwarded to each of the four Archbishops of Ireland on the 16th of January, 1841. After detailing the reasons why the Holy See did not deem it expedient to answer the proposed query by a solemn decision, the Irish Bishops are permitted to adopt the system of Irish National Education under safeguards which are set forth at length. The exact words of the document in English are :—

"How weighty a matter it is which has been
"brought on by the controversy, raised in Ireland
"on the recent National System, as they call it, of
"educating youth, is so well known to your Grace,
"that you ought not to be surprised that the
"answer of the Sacred Congregation *De Propa-*
"*ganda Fide* in reference to that question should
"have been so long delayed. For, Your Grace
"has full knowledge of the whole affair, and all the
"weighty reasons which led to the rise of that
"controversy, and which required a truly pro-
"tracted deliberation on the subject, are thoroughly
"known to you.

"For the protection of the Catholic Religion,

"the advantage of educating youth, the duty of
"gratitude towards the Senate of the British
"Empire, which voted a large sum of money to
"the schools for the use of the people of Ireland,
"the necessity of maintaining harmony among the
"Catholic Bishops, the duty of fostering public
"tranquility, and lastly the fear lest the whole
"money and control may pass, perhaps, into the
"hands of anti-Catholics, ought to make the Sacred-
"Congregation exceedingly anxious to give, as it
"was its duty to do, a long and comprehensive
"consideration to the question proposed.

"Accordingly all the dangers and advantages of
"the matter having been carefully weighed, the
"reasons of the contending parties having been
"heard, and above all having received the gratify-
"ing intelligence that during the ten years since
"this system of education has been undertaken,
"the Catholic Religion appears to have suffered
"no injury, the Sacred Congregation, with the
"approval of our Most Holy Lord, Pope Gregory
"XVI., is of opinion that no judgment is to be
"definitely pronounced upon this subject, and that
"this system of education is to be left to the pru-
"dent discretion and religious conscience of the
"several Bishops; since its success must neces-
"sarily depend upon the vigilant care of the
"Pastors, the various precautions to be adopted,
"lastly upon the experience that will come in

"course of time. However, that so important a
"matter be not dismissed without suitable counsels
"and provisions, the Sacred Congregation has
'thought it right to give, in the meantime, the
"following admonitions.

"Namely.—1. That all books containing any-
"thing injurious either to the Canon or purity of
"the Holy Bible, or contrary to the doctrine or
"discipline of the Catholic Church, ought to be
"removed from the Schools. This, however, can
"be effected the more easily since no rule of this
"System stands in the way; 2. That every effort
"possible ought to be made to secure that the
"teacher who trains the Catholic Schoolmasters in
"the class of religion, morals, and history, shall be
"a Catholic, else no teacher. Because it is unbe-
"coming that a non-Catholic should teach the
"Catholic method of religious instruction, or Re-
"ligious History; 3. That it is much safer that
"secular literature only should be taught in the
"*mixed* schools, leaving to each sect its own
"peculiar religious instruction, than that the funda-
"mental, as they say, or common articles of the
"Christian Religion should be taught exclusively.
"For, it would appear very dangerous to proceed
"in this manner with youth; 4. That the Bishops
"generally and Parish Priests ought to be vigilant
"lest through any cause, injury may come to the
"Catholic children from this system of National

" Education, and that it is also their duty to labour
" earnestly to obtain from the governing board, day
" by day, a better arrangement and fairer con-
" ditions. The Sacred Congregation is of opinion
" that it would also be very advantageous if the
" sites of the schools should be held under their
" power and in their own right by the Bishops or
" Parish Priests. They believe, at the same time,
" that it will be of very great benefit if the Bishops
" should often confer with each other in provincial
" Synods on so important a matter. But, should
" anything adverse happen, it is to be sedulously
" communicated to the Apostolic See that it too
" may provide against it.

" Finally the Sacred Congregation wishes that
" in future the Bishops and other Ecclesiastics do
" abstain from disputing over this controversy in
" the public journals or other publications of the
" kind, lest the honour of Religion, their mutual
" reputation, and Christian Charity be injured with
" scandal to the people."

In keeping with these instructions, Dr. Murray asked Dean Dowley for one of the Community at Phibsboro' to impart to the Catholic young men and women, under training in Dublin for teacherships in the National Board Schools, an easy and simple method of explaining the Catechism. This, Dr. Murray believed, would best secure for Catholic children the principle of "separate religious instruction" upon which the System of Irish National Education had been framed, because the Catholic teachers must be the great factor in carrying out this principle under the direction of their respective pastors throughout the country. Now, it is well known that the most effectual way of conveying religious knowledge to the mass, is to make each truth an object of sense by illustrating it with the account of some impressive fact, taken from the Scriptures, from history or actual experience. This one constituent of any good Catechist, Father Hand possessed in the greatest perfection, and therefore he was sent, at the request of the Archbishop, to the National Board Training School at Marlboro' Street, Dublin. He went there, not as St. Paul came to Athens, to bring the proudest intellects of the age captive to the saving doctrines, that surpass all human understanding, but to teach believing intellects and willing hearts. He came to instruct others how to impart to the ' little children " of Jesus Christ the knowledge of faith And, how divine thus to teach the little ones of our Catholic poor! This is a reflection which must occur to every one who sees these children coming out of the squalid lanes and reeking cellars of this city, or still more when one meets them in some of our remote glens, and in the wild days of December, trooping, against the driving rain, with but little nourishment and scant clothing, to some lonely school-house on the side of the bleak mountain road. To instruct others how to teach these poor children their catechism on an easy and simple plan, was now adding considerably to the labours of Father Hand, but it forcibly reminded him of the Saviour blessing the little ones, and the success that attended his instructions, will never drop out of history, for it has been recorded by a distinguished writer of that time.

About the end of 1839, or early in 1840, a popular and gifted authoress in going over the public institutions of Dublin, paid a visit to the Marlboro' Street Schools, under the immediate management of the National Education Board. Here she was courteously conducted through the various departments by the accomplished Resident Commissioner, the late Sir Alexander M'Donnell, and on entering the Normal School, he introduced her to Father Hand, who happened to be then teaching the Catechism. After a few minutes conversation with the good priest, she expressed a wish to hear him lecture, and Father Hand, under gentle pressure from the Resident Commissioner, at once resumed his teaching. The lady was watchfully interested in his exposition of the Catholic doctrine in hands, but when he began in his own happy manner to illustrate his explanation by the story of a powerful Eastern monarch in the "olden time," she seemed deeply moved. At the close, in coming forward to thank the lecturer, she told how profoundly her heart had been touched by what she heard, and turning towards the priest, sank on her knees to ask his blessing! He assured her not only of his blessing but of his prayers, and humbly begged pardon for having, perhaps, rashly ventured to dilate on Catholic truth in such distinguished Protestant presence. "Oh!" she exclaimed "don't say you "have been rash, for I am grateful, very grateful "to you, and I shall not soon forget your admir- "able explanation as well as forcible illustration of "that beautiful Catholic doctrine." And she did not forget this meeting, for it occupied a prominent place in the account she afterwards published of this visit. It is well to remark that this incident, which must add a new pleasure to the general admiration for Father Hand, has been recorded on the authority of one who had it from Sir Alexander M'Donnell who was a personal witness. Mrs. Anna Jameson is the gifted lady whose name has been mentioned in connection with the scene, but in this distance of time it is very easy to forget a name.

Such remarkable success in the delicate task of explaining the truths of faith could not but be appreciated by a bishop like Dr. Murray, whose voice was ever active in calling his flock in and out to the pastures. His loving eye, which kept the whole field in view, was now bent upon the National Board Training School, within the shadow of his own Cathedral at Marlboro' Street, to regard fondly the young reaper whom he sent into that harvest. Father Hand, therefore, was received with marked attention when he called early one morning in 1840 at the Archbishop's residence on Mountjoy Square, to seek the best counsel he could in reference to an enterprise, pronounced by his friends to be rash in the extreme. The humble priest on entering was nervous and agitated by this disheartening reflection; but Dr. Murray's cordial greeting put him perfectly at his ease. He said his business in coming was to ask his Grace's advice on a matter which was making him very unhappy— namely, to establish at Dublin a college for the education of missionaries to preach the Gospel to every creature, but especially to minister to Irish Catholics abroad, who were dying of spiritual hunger. The idea, he went on to relate, was suggested by his connection with the working of the Phibsboro' Branch of the Association for the Propagation of the Faith. The Annals, published by that Association, he read late into the night, and the stirring sketches which they contained often haunted him in his sleep. Indeed, his much-needed rest was frequently interrupted by startling dreams, touching the sufferings and privations of these missionaries. During the day his mind was filled with reflections on what he had read, and this led him to think of the scattered children of his own race and creed. He found them in the great Republic of America, in Australia, and in many other strange lands, begging the bread of life, but no one to break it to them. He thought of them nearer home, and of the vice and wickedness of the manufacturing towns of England and Scotland—where he heard Irish Catholic parents and children crying for an Irish priest to save their souls. He had long prayed to God for light to be able to send Irish missionaries to rescue these his poor exiled countrymen from spiritual death, and the light came to him in an impulse—to establish at Dublin a college for the Foreign Missions. This divine impulse he ventured to embody in a rough plan, which he would now read, with a fervent prayer that his Grace would extend to it his blessing and approval.

The good Archbishop listened with the keenest interest; but, believing it to be his duty to moderate with wise counsel what seemed to him at first sight a religious enthusiasm, he proceeded to represent to Father Hand the difficulties of founding such a college in a poor country. Buildings were to be raised, furniture to be purchased, professors to be engaged, and assuredly a

grand, a holy, but perilous experiment had to be made. How was all this to be encountered? The earthly, like the heavenly riches, were merely in hope, and even students might be slow in availing themselves of an institution of this kind. In short, the undertaking was, humanly speaking, *a dream.* This pronouncement, coming from so high a quarter, dashed the best hopes of Father Hand. He fondly expected Dr. Murray had known him better, and more highly appreciated his views than to declare them *a dream.* His heart was therefore full, and, gathering into his tone all the gravity and solemnity at his command, he replied, according to Mrs. Tanham's impression, in words like these:—"Well, your Grace, if this be *a dream,* I
"feel bound to state humbly, but seriously, that it
"is a *dream* in which I saw my Catholic fellow-
"countrymen abroad, in the attitude of those Irish
"infants whom St. Patrick saw in a vision, stretch-
"ing forth their hands from the wombs in which
"they were confined, and imploring the holy youth
"to come to baptize them. I, too, have had a
"message from heaven, and therefore my firm belief
"is that God will yet place your Grace by my side
"in carrying out the sacred trust, which has been
"confided to me."

The touching character of these words, and the earnest confidence with which they were spoken, moved the heart of the holy Prelate, who, rising in the shadow of the window, spoke, it may be supposed, to the following effect:—

"My dear young friend, I have wounded you unjustly, for I can trace the finger of God in your heavenly purpose. Go; it is impossible that one so single-minded should fail in the cause of God." From this moment Dr. Murray warmly espoused the proposed College at Dublin for the Foreign Missions, and acting under his advice Father Hand went home to his little cell in the Mission-house at Phibsboro', to mature the following letter, which he addressed on the 30th December, 1840, to every Bishop in Ireland:—

"My Lord,

"Having maturely considered the many and vast advantages, which religion would derive from the existence in this country, of a Catholic College for the Foreign Missions, founded and supported, solely by the voluntary contributions of the faithful; we have resolved to devote ourselves to the establishment and management of such a College, under the patronage of the Catholic Archbishops and Bishops of Ireland.

"We look for no earthly remuneration; our humble labours in this most divine work, shall be gratuitous; we will live in community, and endeavour, with the assistance of Divine grace, to train the young Ecclesiastical Students, both by word and example, in the true spirit of their Apostolic state; and to prepare them, to the best of our power, for the efficient and worthy discharge of the sublime functions of their holy vocation.

"We have communicated with the Superiors of the Colleges for Foreign Missions in Paris and Lyons; we have, moreover, consulted with prudent and experienced clergymen at home, and having availed ourselves of their combined prudence and

"experience, we have drawn up a plan, which to us appears to
"be the best and most effectual, for establishing, supporting,
"and conducting the projected College.

"This plan is to be respectfully submitted to the Archbishops
"and Bishops, when assembled in Dublin, to hold their next
"meeting ; to the end that so great a work of religion
"and charity may commence, with the sanction and under the
"protection of the zealous, and venerable heads of the Irish
"Church, and thus merit the sanction and protection of
"Heaven.

"But in order to afford the Bishops time to give due con-
"sideration to a matter from which so much good is likely to
"result, we have deemed it expedient to apprize their Lordships
"beforehand, of our intention to have our plan in its details
"laid before them, at their next meeting. For this purpose, we
"have taken the liberty of addressing to each Archbishop and
"Bishop in Ireland, a copy of this Circular, which gives a
"general outline of our motives and means for getting up
"and working the new Institution.

"The object, therefore, of this address, is to hasten, as
"much as possible, a work so long and earnestly wished
"for, and one so well calculated to promote the glory of
"God, to extend the kingdom of Christ, and to procure the
"salvation of numberless souls, who should, otherwise, be lost
"for ever, seated as they are, in the shadow of death, and
"having no one to break to them the Bread of Life.

"Almost all the faithful, both clergy and laity, who have
"heard of the intended College, seem most anxious for its
"immediate commencement, and most willing to contribute to
"the utmost of their power towards its foundation and support.
"Many have already promised large donations for that purpose,
"whilst others have signified their determination to establish
"free places in it.

"There are in Ireland hundreds of young men, every way
"qualified, both by nature and grace, for the arduous duties of
"the Foreign Missions, who cannot be provided for at home,
"and who, were the College once opened, would most willingly

"enter it, and cheerfully devote the remainder of their lives to the laborious but consoling duties of these missions.

"Begging your lordship's blessing, we have the honour to be, with profound respect and veneration, your lordship's humble and most obedient servants in Christ.

"Signed on behalf of myself and other clergymen associated with me in this undertaking.

"JOHN HAND.

"*Phibsboro' Chapel House, Dublin,*
  "30*th December*, 1840."

CHAPTER VIII.

THE CHOSEN DIRECTORS.

CONTENTS.—Father Hand's first care to associate with himself a number of learned and holy priests—He required their undivided services without fee or reward—He imposed upon them a rule of life—His notion of their fitness—His reply to a zealous priest who offered his services—Letter of the Abbé Cruice, College Vaugirard, hoping he may yet be able to join Father Hand, and offering suggestions on the proposed Foreign Missionary College in Ireland—The other Directors chosen by Father Hand—Dr. Moriarty's eminent powers—Father Hand's conditions for the admission of candidates into his Foreign Missionary College.

LIKE most men who have a great task to perform, Father Hand had to encounter serious opposition, but the firm belief that his work was of God sustained him against every difficulty. Armed with this confidence, no obstruction stopped him, and his success is a striking proof of how much one man can accomplish in a short time. The good Archbishop Murray also traced the finger of God in the enterprise, and strengthened by his countenance Father Hand began now to make remote preparation for it.

In the original plan sketched by him when his mind was on fire, he wrote:—" Nothing should "be left undone to procure pious, learned, and "experienced superiors and professors for the "new College, whose example, as well as words, "will edify and instruct the young Ecclesiastics, "and form them to virtue—who, in one word, "will give tone and temper to the College. I have "no difficulty in saying that persons capable of "filling these offices can be found, who would be "satisfied with food and raiment, and without "fixed salaries." This statement he afterwards emphasized in the letter from his cell in Phibsboro' to every bishop in Ireland :—" We look," he tells them, "for no earthly remuneration; our humble "labours in this most divine work shall be gra-"tuitous ; we will live in community, and endea-"vour, with the assistance of God's grace, to train "the young Ecclesiastical students, both by word "and example, in the true spirit of their Apostolic "state, and to prepare them, to the best of our "power, for the efficient and worthy discharge of "their holy vocation." This he kept pondering in his heart, and silently but surely prepared to give it effect. He felt the immediate need of a few learned and holy priests, ready to labour with him until the sun set, for no other earthly remuneration than "food and raiment." As no time must be lost in securing this chosen circle, he sat down and wrote some rules to bind its members, for we know, he said, from the Psalmist : "How "good and how pleasant it is for brethren to dwell "together in unity." In the first place, he enjoins the strict observance of community life :—" That " we associate ourselves in form of a *Community* for "the establishment and direction of a College in " Dublin, to be exclusively devoted to the aid of " the Foreign Missions."

Then, the members of this Community are directed to take the word of command in all their important concerns from the Chair of Peter, and to be scrupulously exact in the performance of St. Paul's divine message :—" Obey your prelates, " and be subject to them. For they watch as being to " render an account of your souls : that they may " do this with joy, and not with grief."*

Father Hand, therefore continues :—" 2nd— " That we hereby engage ourselves to be in all " things subject and obedient to our Most Holy " Father the Pope, and to the Bishops for the " time being, in whose dioceses we may be. 3rd— " That we shall in like manner live in perfect " obedience to our general, particular, and local " superiors."

The fourth rule prescribes the practice of the Evangelical virtue of poverty by being like the Apostles :—" Having food, and wherewith to be " covered, with these we are content."† The exact

---

* Ep. to Hebrews xiii. 17.   † 1. Timothy vi. 8.

words are: 4th—"That we shall live in *Community*,
" supplied with everything necessary and becoming
" our state, in sickness and old age equally as in
" health and youth, but without salaries; and that,
" like the Apostles and primitive Christians, we
" endeavour, with the grace of God, to practise
" the Evangelical counsels, and keep inviolate those
" vows, made at our baptism and ordination."

In the fifth and sixth the *giving of Missions* is made part of the work of the *Community*, but it is expressly laid down at the same time that the *Professors* shall have no other charge save that of teaching, in order that their studies may be pursued without interruption and without distraction. Thus in the 5th he says:—"That while
" we devote ourselves to the support and direc-
" tion of the aforesaid College, or such others as
" may be founded in connection with it, such of
" our community as may not be required for its
" routine, be occupied in giving missions of short
" duration in those parishes where the Bishop and
" the parish priests may accept of our humble
" labours, or in some such work of zeal and charity
" as our Blessed Lord may deign to put into our
" hands. 6th—That those charged with the care
" and direction of the College, particularly the
" Professors, be not at the same time encumbered
" with any other occupation which might distract
" them or interfere with the efficient discharge of

"their all-important duties. In the same way
"those engaged in the work of the Missions are
"not to be burdened with the care of the College
"at the same time. This rule, however, will not
"prevent what may be after found useful, if not
"necessary, that is to vary the occupations of our
"members, as for example from the duties of a
"missionary to those of professor, and *vice versa*."

Then he ordains that in the deliberations of the community, charity be scrupulously observed, and all measures of importance be decided by the majority of votes by ballot. 7th—"That all
"matters of importance be determined by a
"majority of the members who have the right of
"voting, and their consent shall be ultimately
"manifested by the vote by ballot. At the same
"time the opinion and consent of all the members
"of the community shall be first taken as far as
"prudence may permit, on the various matters
"to be discussed in meeting. Let the spirit of
"fraternal love, union, and charity be the leading
"feature, and one of the distinctive marks of our
"humble body, and in order the better to secure
"and maintain these necessary virtues in our little
"community, we will cheerfully sacrifice our own
"private feelings and opinions, or rather endeavour
"to have no such feelings and opinions."

Father Hand wished above all that the members of his community be "made a pattern of the "flock from the heart." He therefore required of the Directors to join in the devotions of the College-Chapel at the time of prayer, and in the intervals of recreation, to circulate among the students in order to guide them into a groove of easy conversation. He even wishes them to go with the students into the same dining-hall, eat with them at the same table, and by word and example teach them how to demean themselves there.

"8th.—That we should live as much as possible "like the students, seeing that we are happily re- "sponsible for their being made men of prayer, "meditation, study, industry, zeal, self-denial, and "apostolic disinterestedness. We shall, moreover, "eat with them at the same table, and of the same "food; take our recreation with them; join in "their prayers, meditations, and other religious "duties, thus endeavouring in all things, with the "assistance of divine grace, to inspire them with "the apostolic spirit by our example and instruc- "tion. We shall also exercise them on Sundays "and festivals, as circumstances may permit, in "giving Catechetical instructions to the young, the "poor, and the ignorant, or in some other work of "the sacred ministry, so that when leaving College "for the Foreign Missions they may be men of "solid piety and learning, and already practical, "efficient, and devoted missionaries."

It is, I suppose, now generally admitted that the

untainted integrity required for the Ecclesiastical state is perfectly safe in the pure atmosphere of the Catholic houses of Ireland. Hence the long vacation given in our Catholic colleges do not take away from the holiness of the priesthood. But when there is question of crowding the superior teaching and training needed for the Foreign Missions, into a graduated course of five years— the funds of All Hallows do not afford a larger term—we cannot wonder that Father Hand should expunge the word *vacation* from his original programme. This he has done in the ninth and last of his rules:—9th—" That neither we ourselves " nor the students go home to visit our friends " during vacation; and if circumstances arise " which, in the opinion of the superiors, render " such visits expedient, let them be as short as " possible. The students shall be occupied during " the holidays with the work of acquiring useful " information of various kinds, while their studies " must be directed so as to combine pleasure with " useful knowledge, without interfering with their " recreation.

"We, therefore, the undersigned clergymen, "persuaded of the great *desideratum*, as well as " the great practical utility of such an institution, "and with the humble but confident hope of " promoting thereby the greater honour and glory " of God, our own and our neighbours' sanctification "and salvation, do hereby engage to devote "ourselves to this work of charity under the pro- "tection of the Blessed Virgin Mary, and all the "angels and saints. For this purpose we will "assemble in Dublin during the present year, "before or after the 1st of September, so that we "may be enabled to send immediate relief to some "of those suffering missions, where Catholics are "now encouraged to look to us. In this manner "we shall justify the hopes which our Holy "Father the common Pastor of the faithful enter- "tains in our regard."

Thus, Father Hand's first care was to associate with himself clergymen of education, character, and zeal, such as pre-eminently fit them for the task, and his notion of their fitness he afterwards stated very fully and very decidedly, under the following circumstances.

Issy is a solitude or retreat near Paris, belonging to the great Seminary of St. Sulpice. Father Hand was there in May, 1841, praying and studying the difficult art of clerical education, when he received the offer of a zealous Irish priest to be enrolled on his staff. After grave deliberation, and anxious consultation on the matter with M. Cadugue, Superior of the Solitude, Father Hand, in a remarkable letter, declined to accept him. In so doing, he explained at considerable length, and incisively the nature of the sacrifice he demanded from those who aspired to the holy work of educating those who were prompted, by the courage of Christian heroism to carry the faith into distant lands.

In the first place, he declares the fostering of any family tie, or of any affair of temporal profit, must be abandoned by those who would be worthy of engaging in this sublime office. The conscientious discharge of the duties involved in so high a trust ought to absorb all physical and mental energies, even the very feelings and sympathies of the heart. Now, since the applicant was not prepared to sunder these ties, Father Hand felt constrained, though sorely in need of help at the time, to refuse his services when accompanied by what he believed to be blighting influences.

He gives the reasons why he exacts from his colleagues this painful sacrifice of their undivided services without fee or reward. There is question here of training young missionaries :—" To go forth " and preach the Gospel to every creature," and this is truly Apostolic work. But, to accomplish a work of this kind, there is surely need of an Apostolic spirit, which consists in a complete rupture with worldly gain, as well as earthly honours, or as St. Peter expressed it to his Divine Master :—" Behold we have left all things, and " have followed Thee." All this is admirably put by Father Hand in his answer :—

"My Rev. and dear Friend, I hoped to be able
"to answer your last letter sooner, but many
"reasons prevented, or rather rendered it, I may
"say, morally impossible for me to give you any
"kind of a satisfactory answer until this day. I
"know that what I am obliged to convey will
'surprise you not a little, and, perhaps, cause some
"pain of mind. These apprehensions, I assure
"you, render it painful to me to make this
"announcement, that M. Cadugue, Superior of the
"Solitude, where I am staying since Trinity Mon-
"day, having examined your views, and re-
"commended the matter to God in prayer,
"and having also, in union with your humble
"servant, taken time and pains to ascertain the
"Divine will in your regard, declares it to be his
"firm conviction that you are not called to take a
"part in the foundation of the intended College in
"Ireland. He wished to make known this his
"decision, and convey to you at the same time
"that the want of a vocation to any particular
"work of charity does not in any way lessen our
"estimation of the person who does not happen
"to have such vocation. This I often thought
"myself; but fearing lest I should injure the
"cause if I were to say so to you, it occurred
"to me that I had better wait patiently. I hoped
"that God would so change your and my disposi-
"tions before the time for beginning the work, as

"that we would have but one heart and one soul,
"willing and able to die to ourselves and our self-
"love; to lose sight of ourselves, our own ease and
"convenience; to detach our hearts thoroughly
"from everything not belonging to God or tending
"to Him; from the goods of this world, which
"St. Paul and the other Apostles esteemed as
"dust and freely renounced that they might gain
"Christ. I am now more convinced than ever of
"the absolute necessity all those who may be
"called to take an immediate share in this work
"have of imitating to the very letter the Apostles;
"of renouncing themselves, and of taking up their
"cross. It is a work of God, a supernatural work,
"and consequently to be obtained by supernatural
"means, but if natural means are employed, they
"must be in a manner spiritualized by being re-
"ferred to God, and used in accordance with the
"views of faith."

Having thus defined the spirit of renunciation which ought to animate his colleagues, he goes on to trace it in the labours of St. Vincent of Paul, St. Liguori, M. Olier, the founder of St. Sulpice, and in the splendid monuments they left after them. In perfect honesty he declares it to be his settled wish that the College of the Foreign Missions in Ireland should never exist rather than have it directed by men not possessing this spirit:—
"We must," he says, "admit that the Gospel is

"the same to-day as it was in the time of Christ
" Himself, and that what was then necessary, that
" is to leave all things in order to be His disciples,
" is necessary now also, especially for those who
" would be called to the sublime office of forming
" new and, if possible, perfect disciples of Jesus
" Christ, who, like so many apostles, would carry
" His name and faith to distant nations without
" danger of doing mischief or losing their own
" souls. It was in this spirit all works of the
" kind, which have been blessed, and rendered
" successful by Almighty God have been ac-
" complished. It follows that those who may be
" employed in this work should, at an humble dis-
" tance, endeavour in their manner of life to imitate
" the great servants of God who were employed
" by the Almighty in similar undertakings, as for
" example, St. Vincent of Paul, St. Liguori, and
" M. Olier, founder of St. Sulpice. These holy
" men detached themselves from everything,
" parted with everything, and were living examples
" of all they preached and inculcated, while they
" required nothing from those whom they
" governed, that they themselves did not first
" practise. They were, indeed, poor, or they
" made themselves poor for Christ's sake; they
" were humble, mortified, and obedient. *I would
" rather that the College would never exist than not
" to be a truly Apostolic one,* and its superiors not

"be in all things, rooms, attendance, clothes, food,
"etc., like the students, except in cases where a
"doctor would pronounce special treatment to be
"necessary for either directors or students. I
"must also say that I would be exceedingly sorry
"to see any one having money to join our com-
"munity, unless he first parted with his money
"by either devoting it to the work itself, or other-
"wise disposing of it as his conscience may
"direct."

In conclusion, he acknowledges the want of these virtues in himself, and this deep sense of humility cannot fail to elicit feelings of admiration for his character:—"For me," he writes, "I confess, to my confusion and shame, that "I possess not one of the many virtues which "are so absolutely necessary, and I can only "say that God in His mercy has given me a "desire to possess them, and that I have been "up to the present unfaithful in corresponding to "His calls. All these considerations and others "also make me think that I ought not to be in too "great a hurry to return to Ireland, and that I or "any other one whom God may call to the work "cannot be too well prepared to undertake such "an important task."

Nevertheless, the Apostolic spirit, so well described in this letter, had thoroughly pervaded the soul of Father Hand. He sought it in the lives of the Fathers of the Congregation of the Mission, and he found it in the study of their example during the five years he had been associated with these holy men, mostly in their house in Phibsboro'. Thus he laid the foundation of that influence which he now began to exercise in attracting to him a circle of young priests, rich in promise, and destined to become rich in results. One of the first whom he enlisted in his enterprise was the Abbè Cruice. He was of Irish name, and of Irish blood. His ancestors were, doubtless, among those Irish exiles, who found hospitality and a home with the sovereigns of the continent, and in return left to their benefactors a splendid inheritance of civil and military glory.

When Father Hand came to Paris early in 1841, the Abbè Cruice was finishing his Ecclesiastical studies in the College Vaugirard. He was very young, and yet in the range of higher subjects, in amplitude of sacred learning he had very few rivals among his contemporaries, and fewer still in the science of the Saints. It is not many years since he died, as Bishop of Marseilles, in the odour of sanctity, bequeathing to the French Church the lustre of a great name. He was introduced to Father Hand, who, on a short acquaintance became so impressed with his commanding powers that he marked him out for the first place in the chosen circle of Directors, which he was forming.

The young Deacon, soon surrendered to the earnest pleadings of the holy priest, and promised to join the staff of the proposed Foreign Missionary College at Dublin. On reflection, however, he found it entirely beyond the range of his imperative obligations, and with feelings of the keenest distress at the disappointment he wrote to Father Hand:—

"COLLEGE VAUGIRARD, PARIS.

" MY VERY DEAR AND ESTEEMED FRIEND,

" I have derived too much happiness from the few occasions, "which brought us together, to forget you, and to my mind, you "are so near and so special a friend of Almighty God, that I "cannot help revering and loving you. This introduction is by "way of compliment, and I assure you it is sincere, for I am "too much of an Irishman to pay empty or hollow compli-"ments.

"And now coming to facts, I have learned from the Catholic "Directory particulars regarding the new College which have "caused me great joy. Accept my congratulations, and believe "me that I share in your gratitude to the good God for bless-"ing this work so abundantly. Do, please, write and give me "all the news; tell me the details as to the buildings, the rule, "the number of students, and the spirit that animates them. " I yearn for this information, for though we are separated by a "long distance, I take the liveliest interest in your holy enterprise. "Oh! that I had three or four bodies, and three or four souls. " I would, indeed, leave but one *Cruice* at Vaugirard, and carry " all the others to your feet, to be your devoted servants. But "it appears this cannot be for the present. May God's holy "will be done, and may I thank Him sufficiently for having "disposed things in my regard even as they are. You will "perhaps now read me a lecture, and ask why am I not coming "to join you? I cannot; were I my own master I would do so.

"I will ask you, however to pray for me, and speak to God
"from time to time in my behalf, O! Lord, make of Thy poor
"servant, Cruice, a priest according to Thy own heart, *humble,*
"*crucified; loving poverty, humiliation and crosses.* If God grant
"your petition, I promise you will see me before ten years in
"your holy Institution, labouring by your side, and ready to go
"forth and devote my life to any Foreign Mission you may be
"pleased to send me. This is my heart's dearest wish but I
"bow to the will of God."

Thus tenderly this young saint panted to be with Father Hand. Even the separation, inevitable as it was, did not prevent him taking part in the good work. He offers, therefore, in this same letter at considerable length, practical suggestions "to procure both money and subjects" for the Foreign Missionary College:—

"I have been thinking," he says "or rather I am convinced,
"God has inspired me with an idea that may be useful to you.
"In my retreat I was turning over some plan of helping you,
"and this is what I have found. Your difficulty is not so much
"in getting subjects, as in collecting funds, but my plan will go
"far to secure both. Ten pounds yearly, or two hundred and
"fifty francs, is, I believe, the sum you require for the support
"of one Missionary. Now, twenty five persons each contributing
"ten francs, would yield that amount, and numbers could be
"easily found to give ten francs in the year, by starting an
"Association for this object, on the lines of the one for the
"Propagation of the Faith, but on a much smaller scale. The
"money contributed by its members, should be forwarded to
"the Foreign Missionary College at Dublin, and you could
"allocate it in burses of ten pounds each to the Students of
"your own selection. I am firmly persuaded all good Catholics,
"having the means, would be glad to give this much to send
"forth Missionaries, perhaps to receive the martyr's crown. In
"ten years no doubt, some will be leaving you for countries

"like China, and who knows but they may be called to the
"greatest happiness of all, namely of shedding their blood for
"the faith of Jesus Christ? I believe that among the good
"Catholics of France, Ireland, and England, we could organize
"an Association of this kind, with a yearly collection sufficient
"to maintain over three hundred students. I may be mistaken,
"but what is it that man cannot accomplish, when supported
"by the powerful arm of Almighty God?"

"As to getting students, my idea is that they will come to you
"at the call of prayer. The words of our Blessed Lord are
"conclusive on this head:—'The harvest indeed is great, but
"the labourers are few. Pray ye, therefore, the Lord of the
"harvest that he send forth labourers unto his harvest.' Then,
"these other words of His, contain the true secret of obtaining
"from Him what we ask:—'And all things whatsoever you
"shall ask in prayer believing you shall receive.' I therefore
"send you in this letter, the copy of a short prayer, which,
"though only a year old, has been productive of much blessing,
"and is liked immensely here in Vaugirard as well as at St.
"Sulpice. My dear sister, who has been sent a short time since
"as Mistress of Novices to the Convent of the Sacred Heart at
"Sherrytown, America, promised me to have this prayer said
"daily in her Convent, and she has taken with her quite a
"number of copies. I hope you will make it known in your
"College, and have it extensively circulated there.

"Now, I want you to petition the Sovereign Pontiff, to
"attach the ordinary indulgence to this little prayer, and
"to grant, also, a plenary indulgence, to be obtained four
"times in the year by all the Members of our Association,
"who may go to confession and receive Holy Communion.
"Then, if you could arrange to have a special Mass for all the
"Members of the Association, offered up in your College on
"these four privileged occasions, send me the fact and the dates,
"and I shall have both notified by regular circular to the bene-
"factors, with the announcement that by going to Holy Com-
"munion they can gain a plenary indulgence. These spiritual
"advantages are necessary to kindle the fervour and stimulate

K

"the zeal of the Members of our Association. With this object, I would also suggest that you obtain from the Pope a number of plenary indulgences *in articulo mortis*, granting one to each person who enrolled fifty members in our Association, which is, of course, equivalent to the support of two missionaries. You have now my plan, and I beg of you not to pronounce upon its excellence in a hurry, simply because it has emanated from a friend. Study it carefully; ask God to enlighten you and then write to me. Indeed the scheme may be absolutely worthless, but you will be able to see. I also enclose a little picture with its accompanying slip to keep in your Breviary. Read it and if you approve, remember to join in prayer with eight other persons, under the patronage of the Most Sacred Hearts of Jesus and Mary, and be faithful all your life to the performance of all that is set forth on this little slip.

"In conclusion, I must tell you something of myself. The health of my body is, thank God, very good, but I cannot say so much for the health of my soul. My spiritual infirmities can be counted by the thousand, and I am sorely in need of a cure for all these ills. The evil is that I don't realize the mischief they contain, but God does, and He is pained. Pray earnestly, therefore, to Him to give me light to know myself thoroughly. How happy would I not be, if I were not proud? And yet God has promoted me to Deacon's orders! In fact He has made so much of me, that I am ready to die of love for Him, and of sorrow for having offended Him, though I do offend Him every day. Pray, therefore, my dear friend, for me, and God will be glorified in your prayers. A short time ago I heard of a very beautiful incident. A holy nun wished to die, and her only reason for this strange wish was, that in Heaven she could no more offend her Divine Lord! Do you, then pray that I may no longer offend God, for humble and earnest prayer is powerful to obtain everything. If you secure this favour for me, I will be ready to do anything for you.

"Adieu,

"Yours sincerely in Christ,

"P. CRUICE."

At this same time there were two young priests in Rome, not inferior to the Abbé Cruice in fervour, and true Apostolic zeal. They also yielded to the spell of Father Hand's ardour, when in a few months he went to Rome from Paris. One was the Rev. James O'Ryan, who belonged to a family of considerable standing in the south of Ireland. Being of a sickly constitution he was obliged, as a boy, to leave his home in Kerry for a more genial clime. He went to France, and for twelve years he passed through several Colleges there, nursing his health, and preparing, as well as he could, for Holy Orders. The Cardinal Archbishop of Arras then appointed him to a chair in a Seminary at Boulogne-sur-Mer, but Mr. O'Ryan, finding the duties too exhausting for his limited strength, retired to a house of the Jesuits, at Collége de Vals, Le Puy, where his tutor was the learned Father Gury, S.J., and was ordained priest there in 1840. His eyes were now turned wistfully towards the Dome of Peter, and thither he hastened, to trace under its shadow what is most perfect in the holy calling he had just embraced. In the *Eternal City* after having feasted his mind on the wonders of her seven hills, and his heart on the triumph of the Martyrs over the power of the Cæsars, he entered the halls of the Roman Seminary to refresh himself at the very fountain of Sacred learning. Here he was cheered by the cordial companionship, and fast friendship of a young Irishman, who, some five or six years before, came there from his native city of Dublin, to dedicate himself to God in the service of the altar. This was Dr. Woodlock, the present Bishop of Ardagh and Clonmacnoise. He was ordained priest in the December of 1841, and proceeded in due course to his Doctor's degree, when Father Hand told him the story of the Foreign Missions, and immediately followed the offer of Dr. Woodlock's services.

The Rev. James O'Ryan imitated the generous example of his companion, but he was not long spared to All Hallows. He had a tender frame, and consumption setting in, wasted it out of life in a few years. How Father Hand exercised his powers of fascination on these two distinguished young priests in Rome, is thus told by one of them:—" Father Hand, who reached
" Rome in December, 1841, or January, 1842,
" soon became acquainted with the Rev. James
" O'Ryan, who was attending lectures in the
" Roman Seminary, and with the Rev. Bartho-
" lomew Woodlock, a student in the same institu-
" tion, who had been ordained in December,
" 1841. To these two young clergymen separately
" Father Hand laid open his plans, and early in
" 1842 they joined him in his project, agreeing to
" become members of his intended community,
" and to devote themselves gratuitously to the

"direction of the proposed College for the Foreign
" Missions. The former of these clergymen was
"a native of the diocese of Kerry, but not know-
"ing the Irish language, had taken an *exeat* from
" his diocese, and had been ordained on dimissorials
"of the Cardinal Bishop of Arras, in France, in
"whose diocese he had been professor for some
"years. Rev. Mr. Woodlock was a native of
" Dublin, and had been ordained for that
"diocese."

It is to be regretted that Dr. Woodlock did not write the life of Father Hand. The Bishop of Ardagh was specially fitted for this work, for he had been with Father Hand from the beginning, and was one of the few valued friends who enjoyed his confidence to the last. No man, therefore, knew better where to look for the materials, and there is no one who had more access to all that is known of the founder of All Hallows.

These successes of Father Hand in surrounding himself with able and holy men still continued. In 1843 the Rev. Dr. Bennett, after having graduated with honours in the University of Louvain for seven years, and taken his degree, came home to the house of the Grand Carmelites in Dublin, to which ancient and venerable order he belonged. He soon came within the influence of Father Hand, and in November, 1843, the Rev. Dr.

Bennett, with the permission of his Superior, was already teaching in All Hallows.

But, perhaps, the most eminent name among the Directors whom Father Hand brought to his side, is that of Dr. Moriarty. His soul was pure, like the Lakes of his own Killarney, and thus he came to show an inclination for the priesthood at a very early age. In Maynooth he had a fine reputation, and from a studentship on "the " Dunboyne," he was promoted to the responsible office of Vice-President in the Irish College at Paris. Passing through Dublin at this time he came to see his cousin, Father O'Ryan at All Hallows, and in the course of his visit was so taken with the sublime character of the work in which the Directors there were engaged, that he asked Father Hand for a place among them. This he obtained readily, but his rich supply of acquired knowledge, and native grasp of mind, were not long without appreciation. He is remembered in the College by those who knew him, as the very type of the retired student, and assuredly he had the scholar's temperament, for he was never so happy as when with his books. In the familiar intercourse of his society, his conversation abounded more with weight than talk. He also wrote a good deal, and as the man so were his writings—full of inspiration. A complete collection of his works would interest many readers, for they gladly welcome what has already been published.

To his great intellectual powers Dr. Moriarty added a sound judgment, and a comprehensive breadth of view. Hence, when Father Hand at the supreme moment of his lamented early death, recommended Dr. Moriarty to be his successor, and bequeathed to him the solemn trust of perfecting what was only begun, it was only what could be expected. And this sacred trust Dr. Moriarty discharged with a will, strong to devotion, until he was summoned from it in the end of 1854 by Papal Brief, appointing him Bishop of Antigone, and Coadjutor to the Bishop of Kerry. Dr. Moriarty, when he became President, put, with the assistance of some of his colleagues, into a permanent form, those rules drawn up by Father Hand, which have been described. In a letter written by Dr. Moriarty, and dated June, 1847, from the South of Ireland, where he was staying under medical advice, he thus refers to the wisdom bequeathed by Father Hand in his College rules :—" In revolving and
" planning and discussing these matters we ought
" to separate in our minds our form or rule of
" daily life, and our form or rule of government.
" As to the first, I have often admired the wisdom
" and sufficiency of the rules first drawn up by
" Father Hand. Very little was wanting to them

"but their accurate observance. I have often
"thought of him since my illness, and especially
"in relation to those rules, which I considered of
"little importance, and which I was foremost in
"violating. I recollect one time that we all felt
"strongly the impulse of reform, and met in our
"spiritual conference, with something of the
"restlessness of the old Crusaders, thinking it
"was necessary to explore new lands in quest of
"the Lord. But Father Clarke proved to us very
"plainly that all the evil of which we complained
"could be remedied by simply observing the rules
"we had agreed on." Again, in a letter from
Rome some time after, he mentions the same
thing more distinctly:—"These are only crude
"thoughts, you will turn them over, and say what
"you think. Dr. Pompallier, whom I see often,
"and who speaks to me very confidentially,
"would not wish any change. He says that our
"whole establishment, just as it stands, 'est une
"*idée descendue du Ciel.*' He says that what is
"*unique* in our Institution is that it is destined not
"to form *religious*, nor *Missionaries Apostolic*,
"but to create a diocesan secular priesthood for
"the foreign dioceses and vicariates. This is, I
"believe, what no other Institution of the kind
"has yet thought of. If I mistake not, those who
"go from the *Missions Étrangères* in Paris may be
"recalled by the Superior."

The other members of Father Hand's circle were the Rev. James Clarke, a devoted young priest of the diocese of Waterford; the Rev. Patrick Kavanagh of the diocese of Kildare and Leighlin; and the Rev. James O'Brien of the diocese of Meath. Then came a holy priest from Killaloe. This was the Rev. Michael Flannery, who was afterwards appointed bishop of his native diocese. The last, but not the least, whose invaluable services were secured by Father Hand, was the Rev. Richard O'Brien, D.D., now Monsignor, the Dean of Limerick. He was a highly-cultivated, energetic priest, devoted to the Church and to his native land in everything he said and did. Ireland and her Catholicity have been truly honoured by him, for he has been eminent in the literature, in the eloquence, and in the politics of this country for the last thirty or forty years.

In collecting around him these distinguished Professors and Superiors, Father Hand, as we have just seen, adopted a high standard in judging of their fitness, but for the material they were to mould he had, comparatively, a still higher test of selection. The extracts already given from his early writings show this, and the views meagrely expressed there, he now sets forth at large in a paper, written as a guide for the admission of what he considered the proper class of students.

Dedicating oneself to the heroic work of the Foreign Missions is an engagement with God, which Father Hand believed to possess all the inviolability of a solemn vow. It is therefore an awful responsibility which, to his mind, ought not to be undertaken in a moment of youthful religious impulse, which shifts like the sands on the seashore. A mature judgment is alone capable of weighing all the surroundings of so serious a step, and for this reason Father Hand makes twenty years the age of admission into his College, and requires the candidate to have an *exeat* from his bishop:—"The idea," he says, "of devoting "oneself for ever to a life so painful to human "nature by the numerous sacrifices it imposes, "ought to be maturely considered, and no final "determination be made which might probably be "followed by regret. Moreover, it would be "desirable not to send out missionaries younger "than twenty-five; and, therefore, to save the "limited funds of the College from being over- "taxed, it would be advisable not to receive "students under twenty. Then if candidates were "admitted without an *exeat* from their respective "bishops, many might be tempted to leave the "College, after having received at least part of "a gratuitous education, which would entail an "immense loss to the College. Let us hope, "then, that the bishops of Ireland will save us "from this loss by making it a rule not to adopt "any subject, to whom they have once given an "*exeat*."

Again, to go on the Foreign Missions, means the giving up of home with all its joys and comorts, for a life of extreme privation in the burning heat of the tropics, or the Arctic cold of northern latitudes. A change so severe would be simply fatal to a youth of tender frame, and hence, the student who proposes to enter All Hallows must be, in the words of Father Hand, "of "strong constitution." "Unless a young man," he says, "is free from sickness and debility, he "cannot expect to be of much use in missions, "attended with the most painful labours. It "would, therefore, be necessary to receive candi-"dates physically strong, and with this object to "ascertain by judicious inquiry that they are free "from any hereditary taint of unsound con-"stitution."

Father Hand requires not only the health of the body, but also the health of the mind. The constant labours of the Foreign Missionary leave him but little time for reading. To enable him, therefore, to have the knowledge adequate to the duties of his high and holy profession, he must, while in college, give his attention most thoroughly and his time most economically to long and patient study. Every day, every hour, in fact every moment of the short term of his college course ought to be conscientiously devoted to sacred learning. But this he cannot do unless he enter college with a good share of secular knowledge, and with his reasoning faculties fairly developed. This is why Father Hand assigns such a prominent place on his programme to the entrance examination of his candidates, and to their close attention to professional studies after admission. On presenting himself the candidate "shall," he says, "pass an examination for the "Logic class. Good intentions are not enough "to enable a young man to make himself useful "on a Foreign Mission. He needs, besides, a "competent share of knowledge, and to test "whether he is capable of acquiring this com-"petency he must pass an examination, pre-"liminay to the ordinary course of ecclesiastical "studies. After the great study of perfection "comes that of acquiring a knowledge of science "in order to expound in an intelligent and in-"teresting manner, the Word of God, and "propose to others sound rules of good conduct. "Hence any student, who may not apply himself "so as to give satisfactory proof of his scientific "acquirements, and well-founded hopes that he "will, during life cultivate a taste for study, "should not be kept in the College."

Then the labours that await the missionary in

foreign parts are so wearing and so distracting as to take away, to a great extent, the relish for prayer, especially meditation, because in it more than in any other prayer consists the union of the heart with God. The mere resolve to practise it will effect little in this important concern. In college an inexhaustible supply of earnest, persevering piety must be laid in to draw from, otherwise the keen edge of zeal may be blunted, and the fire of divine love may be cooled. " For this reason " adds Father Hand:—" A student while in our
" College must lay up a store of sincere and solid
" piety, exempt from singularity and weakness.
" The piety of a priest ought to be great indeed,
" but there should be nothing too ardent, too
" demonstrative, or puerile about it. Much that
" could be tolerated in the piety of a person of
" more humble station would be often objectionable
" in a clergyman, and above all in a clergyman
" appointed to direct others. Everything in a
" priest ought to be steady and matured, and this
" applies in a particular manner to priests en-
" gaged in the work of the Foreign Missions.
" Hence in college our students must be taught
" to cultivate a love for the ceremonies of the
" Church, and for everything connected with the
" Divine worship. It is well known that the
" fervour of the faithful is in a great measure
" stimulated by these external rites of our holy

"religion. And this is why all the prelates of the
" Church, and all the great servants of God,
" recommend a scrupulous attention to them. A
" student who does not exhibit an ardent desire
" to know them would be wanting in the first
" mark of a true vocation. In admitting students,
" therefore, we shall be very particular in re-
" quiring a good recommendation from their
" parish priests, for they are supposed to have
" the best opportunities of knowing the life and
" conduct of the young men in their parishes.
" Other respectable persons might with advantage
" be often consulted. Also from the student after
" admission a promise ought to be exacted to
" observe faithfully the discipline of the College,
" in order to become, with God's holy will, a true
" missionary. When first a student enters, it
" would be too much to expect him to declare
" positively that he will go on a Foreign Mission,
" for he may not know all that is demanded of
" him by such a vocation. What can reasonably
" be required of him so far is that he shall not
" enter the College with the idea of leaving unless
" under the advice and command of his Superiors.
" But when he has been in the College some
" time, and is called to Tonsure, then it would
" be well to require from him a formal engage-
" ment never to forsake his first promise. If
" an arrangement had been entered into that no

"student would be ordained unless for a special
"mission, and at the formal request of a particular
"bishop, who would give dimissorials to that
"effect, some ceremony ought to be instituted by
"which in the giving of Tonsure, the student
"would solemnly bind himself to be during his
"life at the disposal of this particular bishop and
"his successors."

Then Father Hand was anxious that the priests educated in All Hallows should be of gentlemanly manners. A disregard for, or an ignorance of the rules of society in a minister of religion, shocks the people in new countries terribly, and even repels them from his sacred ministrations. Father Hand felt this truth, for he sternly insisted on the forms of polite life being cultivated by the students, and upon the directors pointing out to them the mistakes and improprieties more or less prevalent in conduct and speech. We find him, therefore, prescribing among these conditions:—"A bene
"volence of disposition and expression necessary
"to inspire confidence. Let a priest be ever so
"virtuous and well-inclined, if he have not man
"ners sufficiently pleasing to attract those who
"may stand in need of his ministry, he cannot
"hope to do what good ought to be expected from
"a missionary. It is well known that a rough
"temper and unpolished language are the greatest

"obstacles to the respect and love of the people,
"and the priest who does not command the love
"and respect of his people can effect but little
"among them. At the same time the priest
"ought to be without affectation in his dress,
"frugal at his table, and reserved in the matter
"of amusement, since he would otherwise show
"that he was animated by the spirit of the world,
"and not by the spirit of his Heavenly Master.
"To indulge in such vanities would indicate a
"mind not impressed with a due sense of the
"dignity of the sacred office, and surely it would
"not be in keeping with the laborious and painful
"life of a Foreign Missionary."

These were the principles framed by Father Hand for the students who have entered All Hallows since it was opened on the 1st November, 1842, and for the number who went forth from it as priests during that interval of forty-two years. The first sixty of these students were received by Father Hand himself, and they were destined for Agra and Madras, in the East Indies; for Trinidad in the West Indies; for Sydney in Australia; for Scotland; for the United States of America; for Demerara, and for Nova Scotia. Of these first sixty students, twenty-three were ordained priests and sent on their distant missions before

Father Hand's death in 1846, and nearly all of them soon succumbed to hardship, far away from home and friends :—" Being made per-
" fect in a short space they fulfilled a long
" time."

CHAPTER IX.

IN THE SOLITUDE—AT THE FEET OF PETER.

CONTENTS.—Father Hand resolves to go to France for a knowledge of the special method pursued there in the difficult task of clerical training—Letter of Archbishop Murray recommending him to the heads of the Ecclesiastical Colleges on the Continent—Father Hand's sorrow in parting with the priests of the Congregation of the Mission—He is enabled to meet the expenses of his journey by the charity of a friend—His *will*—Excellence of the Sulpician system—Father Hand devoted to it intense study—From it chiefly he framed the Rule of his own College—He spent six months in the *Solitude* at Issy between his cell and a hermitage—The pattern he proposed for the imitation of his Missionaries is the life of the good secular priest—He went to Rome for the sanction and blessing of the Vicar of Christ—While in the Eternal City he sacrificed his undivided time to the cause he had at heart—The prayer of his memorial to the Sacred Congregation of the Propaganda is heard—Archbishop Murray's letter expressing his gratification—Father Hand in special audience with Pope Gregory XVI. who gave him his sanction and blessing—Father Hand published an appeal for support—Cardinal Fransoni, Prefect of Propaganda, sent a flattering report of Father Hand to Archbishop Murray—Father Hand before the Central Council of the Association for the Propagation of the Faith in Paris—Liberal support of the Irish Branch of the Association for the Propagation of the Faith—Their claim to control the Foreign Missionary College at Dublin set aside by Father Hand—A Penny-a-Week Collection organized by Father Hand—After begging successfully from door-to-door in Dublin, Father Hand is generously received by the priests and people of his native Meath.

HAVING thus matured his plan, Father Hand resolved to perfect it by consulting the wisdom and experience of those who had been long and successfully engaged in the difficult task of clerical training. There were also Colleges devoted exclusively to the education of priests for the Foreign Missions, and it would be necessary to become acquainted with their special method. This must be done on the spot, and Father Hand prepared to leave immediately for France and Italy, where he believed the best information was to be found on the subject. He laid particular stress upon this in a remarkable letter, noticed elsewhere at considerable length. This was written to the zealous priest who offered him his services, and in it he said:—" I ought, by all " means, endeavour to see some of the different " societies that direct seminaries, and to endeavour " with the Divine assistance, to acquire even the " rudiments of a religious life, and some know- " ledge of the proper method of conducting an " Ecclesiastical College." It was in search of this knowledge Father Hand arranged to leave for the Continent. Dr. Murray, his good bishop, approved the step, and in a friendly introduction recommended the bearer to the heads of the various institutions to be visited:—

"Daniel Murray by the mercy of God and favour of the "Apostolic See, Archbishop of Dublin, and Primate of Ireland, "to our beloved son in Christ, the Rev. John Hand, priest of "our diocese, eternal salvation in the Lord. It has come to "our knowledge that in furtherance of a laudable endeavour "towards the training of young priests for the Foreign Missions, "it is your purpose to to go and dwell for some time in the "Seminaries and Colleges where this work is going on, so as to "become more fully and more intimately acquainted with their course of studies, their rules and customs. Now, in accordance with your wishes, we hereby make known, and testify that you are a conscientious, orthodox and pious priest, free from all ecclesiastical censures whatever. Moreover, as far as our influence may extend, we earnestly recommend you to all the faithful in Christ, and in a special manner to the heads of Seminaries, to the Cardinals of Holy Church, to the Prelates and other grades of the Ministry. We pray that they receive you kindly, and extend to you their best protection and assistance.

> "Given at Dublin under our Seal and Signature, this 18th day of February, 1841.
>
> "DANIEL, Archbishop of Dublin, and Primate of Ireland.
>
> "JOHN HAMILTON, Archdeacon of Dublin, Secretary."

On the eve of his departure, Father Hand gave unmistakable proof that his heart was sore at the near approach of having to sever a connection which he had fondly hoped would endure during his life. When, under the Divine impulse, he withdrew abruptly from Maynooth five years previously, to join *the Fathers of the Mission* at Castleknock, it did not occur to him, even as a remote contingency, that God had destined him for a more arduous work. But, the Divine will soon pointed out to him a different sphere of action from that of the priests of St. Vincent of Paul. In obedience to this heavenly invitation, he must now go out into the cold world from the warm sunshine of that genuine and lasting friendship which can exist only among men of God. Nothing less than the voice within, speaking under the pressure of Divine command could separate him from a family of holy associates, who reciprocated his genial manner, and cherished him because of his great virtues. We can, therefore, well understand that the parting with these loving companions was a tender one, and had much in common with that affecting scene in which St. Paul bade farewell to the sorrowing Ephesians, who followed him in a crowd to the ship which was to bear him away, weeping and falling on his neck. Even so, Father Hand tore himself from that labourious, but cherished home at Phibsboro', where the first fruits of his ministry were gathered. He was alone and penniless. It is true he had the promise of some £6,750, in donations, for free foundations, from a few generous Catholics. But none of this was available, so that Father Hand was literally without a shilling for his journey until he was about leaving, when he called to say good-bye to his dear friends, the O'Reilly's of Ratoath, in county Meath, who happened to be staying in town, and had taken a warm interest in the object of his journey. Miss O'Reilly accompanied him to the door, and in grasping his hand for the last time, she dropped into it a purse of gold, to help him, as she said, on the way. It proved, however, to be ample provision and more, and strange to say, it was to strip himself even of this charity, he wrote his *will*. This document was composed in a Solitude at Issy near Paris, where he retired some months after this, to be with God alone. Here amid surroundings highly suggestive of the tomb, the thought of passing away took a strong hold of his imagination. In these solemn moments of reflection on death he directed that what remained of Miss O'Reilly's gift, which was not much diminished, should be devoted to the use of the Foreign Missions and other charities :—

"J. M. J.

"In the name of the Most Adorable and Blessed Trinity, "the Father, the Son, and the Holy Ghost.

"I, the undersigned, John Hand, now residing in the Solitude "of Saint Sulpice at Issy, near Paris, and a native of the county "Meath in Ireland, ordained priest at Castleknock, and doing "duty lately in the Sacred Ministry at Phibsboro', near Dublin. "At present in sound health, and in full possession of all my "mental faculties, I do hereby will and bequeath all the "earthly goods I now possess, or may possess at the hour of "my death, both in money and in value, real or personal, "movable or immovable, to the Rev. Mr. McNamara, "and the Rev. Mr. O'Connell—I mean the Rev. Thomas "McNamara of Castleknock, and now doing duty at the Chapel "of Phibsboro'; and the Rev. Andrew O'Connell, parish "priest of SS. Michael and John's Catholic Church—including "sixty pounds sterling, at present in the hands of the Rev. "John Smyth of SS. Michael and John's Church, Dublin, and "lodged by him, as I understand, in the Savings' Bank, Dublin, "as portion of his pass-book account, including also forty-five "pounds I have with me, as also my clothes, books, etc."

No man had stronger affections than Father

Hand, and no man suffered more when these were wounded. He took pains to write to his father and mother frequently, to pay them a visit rarely less than once a year, and in this his "last Will and Testament," as he calls it, he did not forget them. Of "the world's goods" he possessed little, but even in this little he remembered them, and with it left what they prized more, namely the pledge of his affectionate memory. Therefore, he goes on to say:—"Except five shillings, which I will to my "beloved father and mother, mamely Mr. Luke "and Mrs. Margaret Hand, Woodville House, "near Kells, provided they think well of receiving "this small sum in testimony of my love and "remembrance of them, for though I do not make "my will in favour of my parents or friends, this "does not arise from a want of love, affection or "esteem for them; on the contrary I love them as "I do my own soul. It is for conscience sake, "and the love of my own soul as well as those of "my friends, and above all the love of God, that "I have made this my last will."

With the exception of these five shillings to his father and mother, he instructed his executors how to dispose of all the rest in the following private letter:—

Issy, near Paris,
February, 25th, 1841.

"My dear Rev. Mr. O'Connell, and Rev. Mr. McNamara."
"I wish you to dispose of my money and property which I have

"willed to you, in the following manner :—Give ten pounds ster-
"ling towards the building of the Chapel, Schools, and Presbytery
"at Phibsboro'; ten pounds to defray the expenses of the
"country missions as soon as the rev. gentlemen of Castle-
"knock may commence them; ten pounds to the rev. gentle-
"men of Castleknock to say masses for the repose of my soul,
"also for my parents, relatives, friends, and for all those living
"and dead, for whom I am in justice or charity bound to pray.
"I wish you to give three pounds to Mrs. Meredith, the house-
"keeper of the Chapel-house at Phibsboro', during my time
"there; five pounds to the poor about Phibsboro', to be spent
"chiefly among the children of the poor schools to buy beads
"for saying the Rosary. What will remain after paying my
"debts and funeral expenses, I wish to be given to assist in
"establishing in Ireland a College for the Foreign Missions,
"should any persons be found to devote themselves to that
"work in the diocese of Dublin, within the space of ten years
"from this date. If not, I wish it to be given to assist in
"educating some worthy priest for the Foreign Missions, or to
"be handed over to the Committee for the Propagation of the
"Faith, No. 5 Essex Bridge, Dublin, to form a part of the
"General Fund.

"I beg of you to pray, and to get as many others of the clergy
"and laity as you can to pray for your humble and obedient
"servant in Jesus Christ,

"JOHN HAND.

"The Rev. Messrs. A. O'Connell and T. McNamara"

Having arrived in France, he visited every institution in which the vocation to the priesthood was most successfully nurtured, not only for the missions at home, but in a special manner for the more heroic work of the ministry abroad. In each he prolonged his stay until he made himself familiar with the practices by which this perfection of the ecclesiastical spirit was obtained. He also copied their rules carefully, and thus succeeded in storing a large supply of information, when he came to finish the circuit of the French Colleges in Saint Sulpice at Paris.

About the year 1642 it occurred to M. Olier, a holy priest in France, that the best way to effect a permanent reform among the clergy of his own country, was to bring them, during their College course, under the immediate example of a community of secular clergymen, who by their rule would profess the perfection, which ought to mark the life of a priest, engaged in saving souls on the mission. His wonderful zeal in this matter soon attracted to him some devoted priests, whom he formed into a community, consisting of a superior, twelve assistants, and other subordinate members, to represent our Lord, the twelve Apostles, and the seventy-two Disciples. With these in 1645, he opened in Paris an Ecclesiastical Seminary known as the *Great* Seminary, because it is the first in time and in dignity, among the numerous Seminaries of the same class, scattered chiefly over France.

Now every young priest, who wishes to be true to the vows of his ordination, must begin, from the first day he enters on his mission, to act upon a motive, which will be to him a stay and guidance through every step of his career, for life is made up of a series of actions, and without some fixed principle of conduct, he will be borne hither and thither by every wind. But with a right rule he will move straight on, as in a groove, to the crown of a good and faithful pastor. This governing principle is *personal sanctity*, and to train young ecclesiastics to the peristent practice of this in the midst of the dissipating cares of the busy world, M. Oliér made some members of his community responsible for the weighty duties, of the populous and extensive parish of St. Sulpice in Paris. Hence his Society has been called the Congregation of St. Sulpice, and how well it has fulfilled its object, the history of the French Church for the last two hundred years abundantly proves.

Father Hand in examining the constitutions of this Institution was pleased and surprised to discover that in spirit and almost in the letter they corresponded with the outcome of his own thoughts when he first conceived the idea of a Foreign Missionary College. It is, therefore, easy to understand why the rule of St. Sulpice was adopted as his model. Before doing so he made himself familiar with every detail of it. During this long and anxious study he resided in the *Great* Seminary at Paris, and had the good fortune of witnessing the cheerful and exact observance of the rule. This obedient regard for the rule is, perhaps, the most noteworthy feature in the Sulpician system.

It is handed down as a sacred trust in the traditions, which accompanied the growth of the Society from its inception, and seem to have stamped a devotional character on the mind, manners, and entire bearing of every one living under their wholesome influence. The spirit thus transmitted is made to flourish by one of the duties imposed upon the Superior. He is bound in virtue of his office to explain the text of the rule at the beginning of the Academical year, and give a spiritual lecture every week on the obligations it enjoins. This is done so conscientiously and in such a solid, judicious and exhaustive manner, that it may be regarded as not the least important element in the successful working of this admirable organization. Spoken meditations on the holiness of this stern adherence to the rule are also given by the members of the Community in their turn, and thus every Director, to keep himself above suspicion, must practice what he teaches. On these solemn occasions all stand up in pensive attitude to follow the speaker. The effect is very striking, and every one present is deeply impressed by it.

The well-known excellence of the Sulpician system is immensely strengthened by the bond of association or companionship, which unites the representatives of authority with those they govern. The Directors share with the students the same table, and the same crust; they join in the same chapel, and visit them in sickness. In time of recreation, they enter into easy conversation with them, and the students meet this confidence not only by giving their opinions candidly and honestly, but by opening their minds fully to seek counsel. Through the mutual confidence thus established, the superiors are enabled to note the dispositions, habits, and general character of their subjects, without that prying curiosity which repels confidence. The Superiors also while mixing freely and sympathetically with their inferiors, treat them with great respect and politeness, not in a stiff, formal way, but in a cheerful, respectful tone. This example acts as a powerful incentive on the students themselves, to cultivate good manners, and to be ever mindful of charity towards each other. Then, the Directors are not ostentatious of their power, and do not threaten or reprimand, except in very peculiar circumstances. They try never to hurt the feelings of any student, but when it is necessary to administer correction, they do so without passion, calmly, seriously, firmly, and with the most paternal solicitude. The result is that the Superiors and subjects of St. Sulpice have but one mind, one heart, and one spirit, so that every student comes to entertain a warm attachment for the Directors of his college. They may be seen in common, working side by side, in striving after the true ecclesiastical spirit, and both are equally proud of their institution.

All this furnishes a splendid proof, if such were wanting, that the rule of St. Sulpice is founded on the principle of governing, recommended by our Blessed Lord to His Apostles, when He said:—
" You know that the princes of the Gentiles lord
" it over them, and they that are greater exercise
" power upon them. It shall not be so among
" you, but whosoever shall be the greater among
" you, let him be your minister. And he that will
" be first among you shall be your servant." *
What wonder, then, that such a perfect type of ecclesiastical life should be able to win so many extraordinary vocations from the army of France, and from among the best men in the learned professions there? We cannot be surprised to find the Sulpician system regarded commonly as the model of clerical training, and the glory of the French Church.

The next step taken by Father Hand was to shut himself out for a time from distractions, in order to be exclusively with God. It was in these circumstances many of the saints received their best inspirations, and the supernatural power to carry them into effect. Now, there is at Issy, near Paris, a *Solitude*, attached to the *Great* Seminary of St. Sulpice, and Father Hand, with the kind per-

---

* Matt. xx. 25.

mission of the Superior, withdrew to this retreat. Here he lived from early morning till evening late, in the chapel, and in his cell by turn. When he had first implored the light of the Holy Spirit, long and fervently, before the altar, he was busy the rest of the day in writing out the suggestions he received in prayer, on his experience of the various nurseries of clerical education he had visited. In this way the work of years seemed to have accumulated around him in as many months. His little study was literally filled with printed documents, books of reference, and piles of manuscript. This was the description given of his surroundings by a Dublin clergyman who visited him at the time :—" I found," he said, " my holy and dear friend, Father Hand, in the " *Solitude* at Issy, almost knee-deep in parchments, " manuscripts, and books. He seemed regularly " buried in the effort to draw up a constitution, " which will revive the missionary spirit of " Ireland."

In the account, known as *The Confessions*, which St. Patrick has left of himself, he states that while preparing to obey the command of God to evangelize Ireland :—" I arose before day to say my pray-" ers in the snow in the frost, in the rain, and yet " I received no injury." He was then in one of the bleakest spots of this country, and he got up to open his heart to God when solemn silence reigns abroad. He even denied himself the shelter of a roof, and went out on the bare mountain, where he knelt for many hours praying for strength to make him equal to the mission for which he had been chosen. This he did night after night, and according to his own words, in the bitterest weather. Sometimes the snow was falling on him in thick flakes, or the nipping frost was piercing his very bones, or the tempest of wind and rain drove furiously up from the wild glens, and beat upon him with all its violence. "I arose," he writes, "before day to say my prayers in the snow, in the "frost, in the rain." Even so the founder of All Hallows in framing the plan of an institution, destined to transmit the Apostleship, bequeathed by St. Patrick to the Irish Church, went forth in the depths of the night to recommend his mission to God. In the garden of the *Solitude* at Issy there is a grotto or cave, pointed out as the *Hermitage*, and to this Father Hand stole over in the midnight to pray.

From the mountain where he had been thus in seclusion with God for six months, Father Hand came down carrying with him the tables of his laws. These embodied the ordinances of St. Sulpice, modified to meet the requirements of a different nationality. In the terms of the Sulpician constitution, as they have been just set forth, the government and teaching of the students is confided to a Society of priests, who unite, for the love of God, in the noble sacrifice of their gratuituous services, without the vows and other obligations of a Religious order or Congregation. This was copied to the letter by Father Hand, because the life of the good secular priest was what he proposed for the imitation of his missionaries in College, and for their steady practice when they found themselves abroad.

The Ecclesiastic who joins a Religious order or Congregation, and takes its vows, contracts solemn obligations, which, if conscientiously fulfilled, will place him in a higher degree of sacerdotal perfection than if he remained in the ranks of the Secular clergy. But these monastic vows fasten a most serious responsibility on those whom they bind, and are found to be very exacting on the priest, who has "to bear the burden of the day and the heats," of the Foreign Missions. If, then, the life of the good secular priest is the most that can be reasonably expected from the missionary abroad, it necessarily becomes an essential part of his training at home. He must see in College every day this model, reflected in the regular routine of those who are charged with the duty of guiding him unto perfection. It was, doubtless, for these reasons, Father Hand decided on placing his intended College in the hands of secular priests, associated like the Directors of St. Sulpice, and he adopted this course only after protracted and prayerful meditation. St. Francis Xavier, the Apostle of India, belonged to a religious order, not surpassed by any in the *regular* army of the Church. The Society of Jesus, and not a few of the other religious orders as well as congregations, have sent out, and continues to send out, some of the most self-sacrificing labourers in the field of the Foreign Missions. This is quite true; still it is not less true that Father Hand in moulding his missionaries, as he did, into a Diocesan secular priesthood, and not into a regular clergy with monastic vows, produced what Dr. Pompallier, Bishop of Auckland, after a long experience of the Foreign Missions, pronounced to be the perfection of his plan, " *une idée descendue du ciel.*" The rule *des Missions Etrangeres* in Paris, and of other kindred institutions elsewhere, invest the Superior of the College with the power of recalling at will their missionaries. Father Hand rejected this from his system, and in so doing, men like Dr. Moriarty, saw one of the most striking proofs of his singular penetration.

Father Hand copied what he considered most suitable to his own design, in the statutes and practices of the several Ecclesiastical Colleges he had visited on the Continent. But his collection wanted the seal of the Fisherman, the sanction of the Successor of St. Peter, to give it probative force.

M

He would not regard even this general plan to have the approval of Heaven, until it had been blessed by the Vicar of Christ. Accordingly, in the first month of 1842, he left Paris for Rome, to place the framework he had put together at the feet of the Holy Father. On arriving in the Eternal City, he rented a small room in a poor quarter, near the Church of Santa Maria del Pascolo. He was out daily toiling on his errand, except during the few hours of necessary rest. He called upon every one he knew or heard of as having influence, and by his singularly humble manner, combined with commanding earnestness, he succeeded in pressing them into his service. The most active energies in Rome were thus enlisted, and through them high Ecclesiastical authorities began to look with favour on Father Hand's design. In fact his time was so exclusively devoted to the cause at heart, that he had to pass unnoticed the monuments of what is greatest both in Paganism and Christianity, on his path wherever he turned.

Father Hand denied himself a visit to what was nearer and dearer to him than those broken thrones and temples. He was not tempted into the gratification of that longing desire, which, in common with every priest, and, indeed, with every good Catholic layman, he undoubtedly entertained—to see the Catacombs, where the early Christians were driven, to live like moles underground, until they died. He had no time for contemplating in the capital of the Catholic world the many celebrated churches. As an illustration of the sacrifice he made of his undivided time and attention in this respect, it is told of him that one day, after his return to Dublin, he was warmly welcomed by a friend who happened to meet him. "Well," said this gentleman, after some conversation, "what "pleased you most among the wonders of Rome?" The question came in the regular order, and yet Father Hand was observed to be greatly embarrassed by it. To be in the capital of Christendom for nearly four months, and not to have gone to see all its principal churches, palaces, and museums was a humiliating confession. He answered, however, after a momentary struggle, "I am "ashamed to say that I know but little of Rome "after my long stay there. There was so much to "be done, that I could not spare the time to explore "its vast treasures."

By these constant and laborious exertions, Father Hand prepared the way for a formal statement of his project to Propaganda. This he now presented as the petition of a few Irish priests, who have resolved to establish a College at Dublin for the Foreign Mission, with the object of meeting the spiritual destitution prevailing in the British colonies and other foreign countries, where millions of Catholics are without the services of a priest.

These devoted clergymen propose to live in community, and give their services gratuitously to the teaching and training of young priests for these forgotten millions. They are confident that the Irish Catholic people will yield an abundant supply of vocations for this distant field, as well as a generous provision for the intended College. Therefore, they implore the protection and approval of the Sacred Congregation. Such is in substance what is set forth, but the words of the memorial in English are :—

"To CARDINAL FRANSONI, Prefect of Propaganda.

"May it please your Eminence,—We are a few Irish clergy-
"men, who have resolved to make some provision for the
"spiritual distress now existing among the millions of our
"Catholic brethren, in all the British colonies, in America, and
"other countries abroad.

"We propose, therefore, to establish at Dublin, a College for
"the Foreign Missions, and give to its working our services
"gratuitously.

"We are secular priests, who will live in community, and
"devote ourselves by instruction and example to prepare zealous
"missionaries. With the direction of Ecclesiastical studies we
"are not wholly unacquainted. Some of us have even con-
"siderable skill in the matter, and we all promise not to spare
"ourselves in accomplishing a charity which, we firmly believe,
"will make religion flourish in those remote parts.

"We see no difficulty before us as to getting subjects. There
"are at this moment hundreds of young Irishmen, willing to
"dedicate themselves to the Foreign Missions, and quite equal
"in the matter of education to enter our College for the higher
"studies of Logic.

"The voluntary contributions of our Catholic people will,

"we are convinced, supply what may be necessary to found and
"maintain such an institution. That the laity no less than the
"clergy take a deep interest in its success, can be gathered from
"a few of the most prominent names among those who have
"already promised to subscribe. The Most Rev. Dr. Fennelly,
"Bishop of Madras, has offered a sum of £1,500 to establish
"three free places; Rev Mr. Power, £2,500 for five free places;
"Rev. Mr. Doyle, £500 for one free place; two laymen,
"£1,500 for three free places; Very Rev. Dr. Yore, Vicar-
"General of Dublin, a donation of £100, and his library;
"Rev. Mr. M'Evoy, a donation of £100; Rev. Mr. O'Reilly,
"a donation of £100; Rev. Mr. Smith, a donation of £50;
"Mr. Daniel O'Connell, a donation of £100; Miss B. O'Reilly,
"a donation of £100, and anonymous a donation of £100. or
"a total of £6,750. These and others, whose names we need
"not mention, came forward without being asked, and the
"circumstance that they have done so much makes, we think,
"our prospects of support still more encouraging.

"The Most Rev. Dr. Murray, Archbishop of Dublin, is in
"thorough sympathy with our object, and His Grace, with that
"characteristic fervour which distinguishes him, has given to it
"the great weight of his sanction. But, to bring down upon
"our undertaking the best blessings of Heaven, and the more
"effectually to insure its lasting success, we beg your
"Eminence to be graciously pleased to have our College at
"Dublin for the Foreign Missions admitted into the protection
"and approval of the Sacred Congregation of Propaganda
"Such is the prayer of John Hand, of the diocese of Dublin, and
"the other priests associated with him in this good endeavour."

Father Hand lodged this petition in the Secretary's Office on the 3rd February, 1842. About the same time he learnt from the most reliable source that the prayer of his memorial would be certainly granted, and in an impulse of joy he wrote to his patron and dear friend, the Archbishop of Dublin, mentioning the fact, The good news was acknowledged by Dr. Murray in a letter which begins with the assurance of His Grace's sincere satisfaction.

"MOUNTJOY SQUARE, DUBLIN,
"25th February, 1842.

"REV. DEAR SIR,

"Your letter of the 8th instant has afforded me the most "heartfelt satisfaction. It has anticipated the wishes of the "Dublin Clergy, and exempted me from the necessity of "applying to the Sacred Congregation, in their name and my "own, for the approbation, which you have so happily obtained, "of our projected College. I will communicate this intelligence "to the Central Council of the Association for the Propagation "of the Faith in Paris, and I fully expect that those zealous and "devoted men will at once see the expediency of allowing us to "allocate, for the support of the projected establishment, a "portion of the funds which are collected *in this Kingdom* for "the propagation of the Faith.

"In the meantime it would be desirable that, with the aid of "Dr. Cullen, you should endeavour to obtain from the Sacred "Congregation a recommendation to that effect. This obtained, "you could, on your way home, have a personal communication "with the Central Committee at Lyons and Paris, whom you "will, I have no doubt, find perfectly inclined to give every "encouragement in their power to a work which is so much in "harmony with the great object of the Association for the "Propagation of the Faith."

The Archbishop concludes by announcing a fact which he is sure Father Hand will be glad to hear :—

"You will find," continues the Archbishop on the other side, "the resolutions to which I have alluded in the beginning of "this letter ; and from them you may conclude with what satis-

"faction the framers of them received the account of your "communication at a subsequent meeting on yesterday.

"It will give me great pleasure to hear of any future progress "you may make. Present my regards to Doctors Cullen and "Kirby, and

"Believe me to remain,
"Rev. dear Sir,
"Very faithfully yours,
"† D. MURRAY.

"Rev. JOHN HAND."

In the *Resolutions* enclosed by the Archbishop, it is declared in few, but forcible words, by the Committee of the Irish Branch of the Association for the Propagation of the Faith, that the Christian religion could not be better promoted than by establishing near Dublin a College for the Foreign Missions. They earnestly hope their President, Dr. Murray, will immediately forward this declaration to the Central Council of the Association in Paris, and employ his great influence in having this College confirmed by the Holy See :—

"1. Resolved—That his meeting is of opinion that the estab-"lishment of a College for the education of Priests for the "Foreign Missions would be of the first advantage to Religion, "and well calculated to assist this Society in its efforts to propa-"gate the Faith in foreign countries.

"2. Resolved—That in the opinion of this Committee, the "vicinity of the Metropolis would be the most desirable locality "for such a College.

"3. Resolved—That these resolutions be enclosed by our Sec-"retaries to the Most Rev. Dr. Murray, our President, and that "His Grace be respectfully requested to aid us in these views, by "procuring the sanction of His Holiness for the establishment

"of this College ; and, at the same time, be prayed to commu-
"nicate these proceedings to the Central Council in Paris.
"Signed, W. YORE, V.G., *Chairman.*
"A. O'CONNELL, P.P., *Secretary.*"

Three days after the receipt of this encouraging letter and enclosure from Dr. Murray, the following *Rescript of Approbation* was despatched from Propaganda by official messenger to Father Hand:—

"Rev. Sir.—" You may easily conceive with what pleasure "the Sacred Congregation has received the memorial which you "have lately submitted to it, for it must be known to you that there "is nothing more ardently wished for by the Sacred Congrega-"tion than that the number of priests, who may be destined to "discharge efficiently the duties of Apostolic Missionaries, be "daily increased. For now that the Missions are so numerous "and extensive, nothing can be better timed than the establish-"ment of such houses, by which it may be effected—that as "'the harvest, indeed, is great, but the labourers few, the Lord "'of the Harvest' may, from those houses, 'send labourers "'into His harvest.'

"Finally, what must confer the greatest honours upon the "same house, and be a peculiar incentive to have so holy a "project carried on prosperously, it is my most agreeable duty "to give you the certain assurance that our Most Holy Father "Pope Gregory XVI. himself has most cordially given, in the "Lord, his highest approbation to the design of establishing "that house ; and, that in order to secure the more abundant "fruits from it, he has most affectionately imparted to you and "your associates his Apostolic Benediction.

"In the meantime, I pray God to bestow on you every "blessing.

"*Rome*, from the College of the Sacred Congregation of the "Propaganda, 28th February, 1842.

"Yours faithfully,
"J. Ph. Cardinal Fransoni, Prefect.
"To the Rev. John Hand."

The Pope, who had been kept regularly informed of these proceedings, appointed a special audience for Father Hand. He wished to speak with one who had originated a movement on the part of Catholic Ireland to further the mission entrusted by Christ to His Apostles. The poor priest came and knelt at the feet of the Sovereign Pontiff. He related how the idea of the Foreign Missionary College at Dublin grew, and assured His Holiness that it would be easily fed by vocations from among the Irish Catholic youth. He described his close attention for the six months before to the study of the systems pursued in the best colleges for educating missionaries. In short, he detailed his views, hopes, wishes, and added that what remained to breathe vigorous life into his endeavour was the voice of St. Peter's successor. The Pope, struck by the humble appearance but forcible speech of the man, marked him out instantly as one of those raised up by God, from time to time, to astonish the world. He spoke to him, therefore, in a hopeful tone of his conception, but to give it life, and above all to maintain it in healthy existence, would require pecuniary resources of large extent. "Great "Pontiff," said Father Hand, "I have these "resources in the traditional charity of my country "towards the propagation of the Faith, and I am "confident it will be equal to this call." "Well, "then," said the Holy Father, "I see you have a "burning love for our divine Lord, a brave heart "to undertake a most difficult task for His sake. "This is a great happiness to me, and I gladly "give you my blessing and my sanction."

We can imagine the flood of consolation which Gregory XVI. poured into Father Hand's soul by these words. We may be assured that at this moment, when he received the blessing of the Vicar of Christ, he was as confident of success as when he afterwards contemplated the throng of students in the halls of All Hallows.

Father Hand lost no time in applying this sanction and blessing to the mine of Catholic charity. He drafted an appeal, setting forth his claims on the alms of everyone having the Propagation of the Faith at heart. The English-speaking populations over the world must remain without priests, unless Catholic Ireland supplies them. This is the burden of his argument, and he does not hesitate to enforce it by saying that, humanly speaking, there is no other country capable of providing these missionaries. This draft he submitted to Cardinal Fransoni, Prefect of Propaganda, who directed him to have it printed, and suggested that Monsignor Cullen, Rector of the Irish College, should superintend its passing through the Propaganda press. His Eminence also sent a subscription of £40, and a large consignment of valuable books for the nucleus of a College library, and, in taking leave of him, put into his hand a letter to Archbishop Murray, containing a flattering report of Father Hand's stay in Rome, and of his interesting negotiations with Propaganda:—

"MOST ILLUSTRIOUS AND REVEREND LORD,

"I am happy to be able to send your grace the most favour-
"able report of one of your priests, Rev. John Hand, the bearer
"of this letter, who is just setting out for Ireland. During his
"sojourn here in the Eternal City, the life he led, and the example
"he gave, have been undeviatingly those of a holy priest.

"His project of establishing a College for the Foreign
"Missions, in Ireland, after receiving the most anxious consider-
"ation from this Sacred Congregation, has obtained our formal
"sanction. The Rescript of Approbation, which the bearer will
"show your Grace, is the best assurance I can offer that the
"success of his undertaking is near to the heart of this *Sacred
"Congregation.*

"Praying God earnestly for a continuation of your Grace's
"health and happiness.

"I remain,

"Your Grace's most obedient Servant,

"J. PH. CARD. FRANSONI, Prefect.

"Most Rev. Dr. MURRAY,
"Archbishop of Dublin.

"Rome—from the Buildings of the Sacred Congregation of
"the Propaganda, 16th April, 1842."

Father Hand left Rome on Monday, 18th of April, 1842, and during the interval between this date and the 4th of June, the day of his arrival in Dublin, he made his subscription list to swell considerably. In passing through Lyons and Paris, he waited, according to the instructions of Dr. Murray, on the Central Council of the Association for the Propagation of the Faith, to ask their assistance. The members of the Council offered him their best wishes, but declined to allocate any sum by way of grant, on the grounds that no Missionary Institution in Europe had been helped so far from the funds of their Association. At the same time they proposed to supply an outfit and travelling expenses to every missionary he could send out.

It is hardly necessary to state that this decision of the Central Council of the Association for the Propagation of the Faith caused Father Hand feelings of the keenest disappointment. He firmly believed it was not a well-grounded judgment, for he said in words quoted elsewhere :—" Twenty "pounds expended here in Ireland on the education "of a young priest for the Foreign Missions, would " go farther to propagate the Faith among the nations " abroad than *one hundred* pounds sent off to these " Missions." He determined, therefore, not to abandon his claim without a struggle, and, accordingly, instigated by his characteristic steadiness of purpose, which was never conquered, he again stood before the Central Council of the Association at Paris in 1844, and thus pleaded his cause :—

"GENTLEMEN,

"It is now some two years since I had the honour of appearing before you, in reference to the establishment in Ireland of a College for the Foreign Missions, which had just received the sanction of the Cardinal Prefect of Propaganda, and of His Grace the Archbishop of Dublin.

"Since then the undertaking has not only been commenced, but advanced beyond my most sanguine expectations.

"On the 1st November, 1842, we opened the College, called it All Hallows, and it entered upon its career *All Saints' Day.*

"Towards its support we have received £5,000 or 125,000 francs from the charity of our good faithful people.

"It is in charge of a community of six zealous priests, who are giving their services gratuitously, and following the rule of the *Great* Seminary of St. Sulpice.

"During the Academical year now closing, the classes of Dogmatic and Moral theology, Mathematics, English literature and Modern languages were in full operation, and attended by 50 students. The candidate on his entrance is obliged to pass an examination in Latin and Greek.

"Every student who promises to accept the mission assigned to him, pays £10 or 250 francs for the year, including the vacation months, which must be spent in the College. There are some excellent students, who can hardly afford even this trifling sum.

"Such, gentlemen, is the *actual* position of our College. As to its *future* success we have every reason to be hopeful, seeing that it is under the attentive supervision of the Archbishop of Dublin, and his Vicar-General, the immediate administration of a community of earnest and learned priests, with whom I have the privilege of being associated. Moreover, it enjoys the confidence of numerous Bishops and Vicars Apostolic, chiefly from Scotland and the British colonies, the protection of the Propaganda in Rome, the approval and blessing of the Sovereign Pontiff. All this ought, surely, to inspire well-grounded hopes that from among the many

"vocations in our country, the College cannot fail to send
"forth a large and constant supply of holy priests to the Foreign
"Missions.

"Gentlemen, the generosity of our Catholic people has,
"without doubt, produced marvellous results. But, it may be
"over-taxed, and we are afraid of falling into this extreme.

"We, therefore, beg you to consider seriously our claims, and
"to help in our pressing wants By extending to us your
"countenance and support, the public confidence in our work
"will be greatly strengthened, while, assuredly, you will be ad-
"vancing the Propagation of the Faith in the very best manner.
"Believe me, gentlemen, there is no more powerful agency
"in this respect than Catholic Ireland, speaking the language of
"Protestant England. Yes, she has a glorious mission, and we
"beseech you not to refuse her your assistance in accomplish-
"ing it.

"Allow me, gentlemen, to remain with the highest regard,
"Your very humble Servant in Jesus Christ,

"JOHN HAND,
"*President of the College of All Hallows.*"

This able and forcible appeal elicited for Father Hand nothing more than the same polite attention as before, and the same barren reply. It was not until 1847, the year after Father Hand's death, that the Central Council of this Association was induced to assist the work done in All Hallows for the Propagation of the Faith. This happy result was effected by a humble, but forcible petition from Dr. Moriarty, who succeeded Father Hand immediately as President of All Hallows. This memorial was accompanied by a few lines from Archbishop Murray, and was answered by a grant of

£1,000, a small sum, considering the work done. One cannot help wondering at this action of the Central Council of the Association for the Propagation of the Faith, when such vast sums are freely given every year by the United Missionary Societies of Great Britain and America, for the diffusion of error in the British colonies of India, Africa, America, and Australia. These societies, which are the active and wealthy Propaganda of heresy, Ireland has to meet single-handed, by sending Catholic missionaries into these countries, and keeping up at the same time a large supply of priests to England and Scotland. The Central Council of the Association for the Propagation of the Faith, one would think, ought to know this, and to remember that unless missionaries are furnished largely by Ireland, many millions of English-speaking Catholics must be exposed to spiritual ruin.

These facts, however, were felt and fully appreciated by the Irish Branch of the Association for the Propagation of the Faith, for while Father Hand was still in Rome it passed those very practical resolutions in his favour, which have been noticed, and, on his return to Dublin, joined earnestly in the immediate preparations for inaugurating the Foreign Missionary College. The Archbishop of Dublin gave the tone. It was, no doubt, under his gentle pressure that a Sub-Committee of the Irish Branch of the

Association was appointed to co-operate with Father Hand in securing a good building near Dublin for the College, and in raising the money necessary to equip and maintain it. The Sub-Committee threw themselves into the work with a zeal which was truly admirable; and by drawing liberally on their own time, as well as on the funds of their Central Committee, they were not long in making splendid progress. Soon, however, the Central Committee began to claim the control of the College, on the grounds of voting most of its supplies. This was not in harmony with Father Hand's views, while it aimed a mortal blow at the plan which cost him so much watching and prayer, and so much labour. He believed, and rightly, that his institution would not long survive the unwisdom of making its teaching and internal administration dependent on an irresponsible body, who had little knowledge, and less experience, of so difficult and complicated a task. So convinced was he of this, that it is more than probable he would have forfeited every penny the Committee was giving him rather than yield to their demand. "Father Hand," said Archbishop Murray, to him at this time, "you must be the Committee yourself." But, among the many powers which Father Hand concealed under a modest exterior, was a considerable skill in tactics. Now, the art of listening is not the least useful in the tactics of debate; and Father

Hand was neither an indifferent nor an inattentive listener, when the question of governing the Foreign Missionary College came on for discussion in the meetings of the Central Committee. He heard the arguments by which it was sought to wrest from his hands an authority, without which the Foreign Missionary College in Ireland could not long exist, but he would not repel them, though sorely tempted to do so. His voice, in fact, was so little heard, that the advocates of this adverse policy supposed he was in its favour; and, not suspecting any opposition, they ceased to discuss the matter. A day, however, had been fixed for the decision of the Central Committee on the question, and when it arrived they were not a little surprised to hear a member of their body move a resolution to the effect that the claim set up by that Committee, in reference to the Foreign Missionary College at Dublin, was opposed to the best interests of the institution. This startling resolution, after a protracted debate, was carried by a majority. Father Hand listened throughout, and by great strength of will he succeeded in concealing his deep mental anxiety so completely, that the strongest advocate of these pretensions would not have suspected how much he felt. Thus he saved All Hallows from a great calamity at the very outset, while he established it firmly in the support of the Irish Branch of the Association for the Propagation of the Faith. It is, however, fair to add that in bringing about this fortunate result, he was aided immensely by an influential member of the Central Committee, whom he had taken into his confidence. This was Canon Pope, of Saint Andrew's, Westland Row, who has had no small share in the advancement of the Catholic religion in Dublin during the last half century. He was a true friend and admirer of Father Hand, and holds him in affectionate memory.

But, perhaps, the most substantial assistance that came to Father Hand at this time was from the penny-a-week collection, which he organized most effectively among the struggling portion of the Dublin population. He divided the city into districts, which were placed under active committees, taken from the most sympathetic he could find among the families of the small shop-keepers and intelligent artisans. These went round during the week, collecting the pence of all within their respective districts, and met Father Hand on the Sunday, to render an account of their stewardship, and receive his further instructions.

The wealthy Catholics in trade, as well as in the learned and other professions, were solicited by Father Hand in person, and while many of them were ready with their genial welcome and money too, some were *not at home* for him. Father Hand's name, however, was at this stage of his public career but little known in Dublin. The fame of his sanctity and his great deeds had not yet spread. Thus unknown and unnoticed, he one day called on a leading Catholic of the city, for a subscription. This gentleman on getting his card, and suspecting his business, sent him word that he could not by any possibility see him just at present. He thought no more of the circumstances, but after an hour or more in passing out, he saw a clergyman, very pale, with spare figure, scantily clothed, sitting in the hall, and waiting. In the present instance the rich man had a tender heart, and it sank within him at the sight of the poor priest, waiting long in so humble a place, and without a movement of discontent. The beggar had not the sores of Lazarus, but he exhibited the patience and meekness of Lazarus! "I feel thoroughly ashamed," this good Catholic gentleman used to say as he often related the incident, "when I think of having treated with "such want of consideration a priest like Father "Hand."

Smithfield was also rich in contributions to Father Hand, and there he was punctually every market-day, going among the honest graziers, who cheerfully opened to him their purses. In this interesting way he begged and continued to beg from place to place, from door to door, until it occurred to him that he was excessive in his demand on the unfailing charity of Catholic Dublin. He now turned to the priests and people of his own native Meath, and they accorded him a most liberal reception. He was the more grateful for this generous response, because he felt it to be unfair to throw upon the 'willing Catholics of Dublin the burthen of an establishment in which, as a common benefit to religion, all Ireland should be interested and take a part, and to which even from selfish motives, and from a sense of justice, all the rest of this empire should contribute. By persevering in this wearying round of begging he collected, in the three years, seven months and two days, he was spared to All Hallows, the sum of £7,500, and from this he continued to pay during that time, the rent of a large house and grounds near Dublin, to make expensive repairs, build some additions, contribute most of the money required for the support of a growing College, and at his death leave on hands £2,500. And thus God continues "to multiply for so many the five "barley loaves and two fishes," by the hands of His servants !

CHAPTER X.

THE FOUNDER OF ALL HALLOWS AND THE TRIBUNE OF THE IRISH PEOPLE.

CONTENTS.—Father Hand asked the Irish Bishops to become the Patrons of his proposed College—They were afraid of doing so without security for its support—By prayer Father Hand converted this disappointment into increased confidence in the success of his undertaking—He found a place admirably suited for the home of his College—O'Connell, the Apostle of Religious Freedom for Irish Catholics—He espoused the cause of Father Hand—His interview with Father Hand—All Hallows is opened with one student on 1st November, 1842—Is is only a part of Father Hand's comprehensive scheme—Father Hand's purpose of attaching to the Missions a Teaching Order of Brothers and Sisters—Irish Catholic Emigrants the first object of Father Hand's solicitude—Necessity of Father Hand's Missionaries accompanying the Emigrants to their destination—In this the Catholic Bishops of America invite the co-operation of the Irish Bishops—All Hallows not yet able even to *follow* the Emigrants with Missionaries—Much to be done in order to complete the work marked out for it by Father Hand—Spiritual destitution of Irish Catholics in the British Army and Navy—Striking illustrations of this in the recent Egyptian Campaign of 1882—The duty of Father Hand's Missionaries in this matter.

IT was one of Father Hand's first cares to get his Foreign Missionary College admitted into the favour of the Irish Bishops. He lost no time in making them its patrons, and sending to each a circular with the heads of his plan. He also asked for an interview, which they appointed for their next general meeting in February, 1841. On this occasion he stated with uncommon plainness the reason why his project was destined to save the souls of thousands—it might be millions. He pointed out the vast field it offered for the unemployed missionary vocations which needed only proper direction to be made a blessing to our people at home, and bring relief to the Catholics of all the English-speaking colonies, who were dying of spiritual famine over the world. He concluded with an exhaustive explanation of every detail of his plan. He was listened to attentively, but not without much misgiving.

When he had done, a few of the Bishops pressed him with questions. He was asked with great directness how he could reasonably hope to raise £6,000 a-year for the support of his proposed College. It was a formidable expenditure which must go on increasing with the growth of the institution. Where was the money to come from? Did he ask the Bishops to sanction an enterprise which was threatened with insolvency in a few years? Such a contingency would be disastrous and disgraceful to the Irish Church. Had he any guarantee against it? "Yes," said Father Hand, in reply, " I pledge myself to raise this money with "the help of Almighty God, who is able to make " the weakest energies accomplish the most arduous " undertaking; and I offer you the charity of Irish

"Catholics *as my security.*" It is not necessary to add that no more questions were asked, but when Father Hand withdrew, his statement was timidly considered. The Bishops, with some few exceptions, were of opinion that they ought not encourage this project, since it was beset with the weightiest pecuniary risks in a poor country like Ireland.

A day or two after, Dr. Cantwell, the Bishop of Meath, in a conversation with his secretary, alluded to the interview:—" Well," said he, " we had " Father Hand before us at our meeting " in Dublin, to hear him on the subject of " his Foreign Missionary College. I listened " with pleasure to his modest, but able state- " ment, and was perfectly satisfied with its con- " clusions. Still, from what I saw and heard around " me on the benches, I am convinced that every " Bishop there, except Dr. Murray and your humble " servant, had the strange notion that the balance of " Father Hand's reason was disturbed by his exces- " sive zeal, and consequently his judgment could not " be trusted in an affair, involving the gravest con- " sequences to religion."

That such was the estimate the Bishops had formed of him, Father Hand knew well on leaving their presence. He felt, therefore, as if some great sorrow had darkened his soul, and walking straight into the church he knelt at the Altar of the Blessed Sacrament.

It was late that afternoon when he went back to Phibsboro'. He told his brethren there of the reception accorded him by the Bishops, but added, in high spirits, that after the interview, while praying for his Foreign Missionary project, he felt a sense of confidence in its success such as was never before experienced by him. The present Archbishop of Toronto—Dr. Lynch—spoke feelingly of this incident not very long since, while expressing his love and profound respect for the memory of the founder of All Hallows. His Grace, when in Ireland a few years ago, renewing his pilgrimage to her holy shrines, came often to pray at the grave of Father Hand. And, indeed, the voice of the public testifies to the uniform sanctity of Father Hand. May this voice be soon answered by an authoritative pronouncement from the head of the Church, that John Hand practised virtue in an heroic degree, and that his sanctity has been judicially proved.

Father Hand, though not prepared for this strong rebuff of the Irish Bishops, saw immediately the grounds of its justification. That the establishing in Ireland of a College for the Foreign Missions would revive her ancient glory of spreading the light of the Gospel, was regarded as certain by the Irish Bishops. They felt, therefore, solemnly bound, in virtue of their high office, to see that this movement be safe-guarded, as far as possible,

against the danger of collapse. They had no assurance of Father Hand's financial abilities. Indeed, all they did know of him, created an awkward suspicion that the enthusiasm with which he was pursuing this object, obscured his vision of the merely human element. So long as the Bishops were in this frame of mind Father Hand could easily understand why they were shy of accepting any connection with his design. He expected, however, their distrust would quickly pass away, and in the meantime he tried to lean upon them, but they shook him off. The reports which he forwarded them regularly were not acknowledged, and he went down to his grave, unheeded, unnoticed and repelled. The first recognition extended by the Irish Bishops to the work of Father Hand came on the 10th November, 1846, nearly six months after his death. in a resolution passed at their meeting in Dublin to this effect:—" Re-
" solved that the assembled Prelates feel much
" gratified at the progress of the Missionary College
" of All Hallows, and that they wish the establish-
" ment continued success."

This attitude of the Irish Bishops was a bitter mortification to Father Hand. He did not give way under it, but threw himself into the work with an additional energy which made it advance by leaps and bounds. His onward course bristled with difficulties, capable of checking the stoutest heart, but his power was from above, and with this he swept aside every obstruction. At length he stood upon a spot, admirably suited in every way, for the home of his proposed College. This was the old Manor-house of the Coghills on the northern suburb of Dublin, near Drumcondra. It is situated in the centre of extensive and well-wooded grounds, which before the suppression of religious foundations in Ireland, belonged to the Monastery of All Hallows. It was Corporation property, and the great O'Connell happened to be Lord Mayor of Dublin for that year. He surely would be happy, thought Father Hand, and he was right, to exert his powerful influence in favour of a cause, which had already excited his warmest interest and obtained his first donation of £100. And, since this great man espoused the cause of Father Hand with all the enthusiasm of his generous soul, and all the power of his persuasive eloquence, he demands more than a passing notice here.

O'Connell was sent to France for his education, denied him by the law at home. Here his giant intellect ripened early, and returning to Ireland he proceeded his call in due course, and rose rapidly at the Bar. From the Bar he passed to the Senate, where his entrance was blocked by a penal statute, bidding him renounce his faith or retire, but a wave of eloquence, rushing from his tongue like a torrent from his native mountains in Kerry, swept the barriers, and from that time Catholics began to have a voice in the Government of their country. Wealth and high place were soon at his command, but he pushed them back, that he might be free to consecrate his splendid genius to emancipate the Church which his forefathers bravely defended until crushed by overwhelming numbers they were stripped of their fair lands, and banishd into the poorest corners of their ancient heritage. From one of the most beautiful of these mountain solitudes O'Connell came forth to change the defeat of his forefathers into victory without the loss of one drop of blood, and to raise Ireland to a place among the nations. He became the *Tribune* of the Irish people, and the glamour of his patriotism spreading abroad, he was everywhere recognised as the apostle of religious freedom. It was a title he well earned, for no oppression is more cruel than to force or bribe a people to act against their conscience, and he rescued the millions of Irish Catholics from this bitter wrong. He emancipated the Catholic laity of Ireland—a stern uncompromising race, who spent freely of their blood and treasure, rather than yield to force or bribe in the matter of their religion, and they became true confessors for the faith. He emancipated the devoted bishops and priests of Ireland, who were ever the strenuous defenders of free altars, and in

this they did but deliver the message with which every priest is solemnly intrusted at his ordination:—" I rise with a recollection that will not
" leave me. When the *priest* in former days rose
" amid the people, something which excited a pro-
" found love rose at the same time with him.
" Now, accused as I am, I know that my name of
"*priest* is mute for my defence, and I am resigned
" to it. The people deprived the *priest* of that
" ancient love, which they bore him, when the
"*priest* deprived himself of an august part of his
" character—when the man of God ceased to be
" the man of freedom. I never knew freedom
" better, than the day when I received with the
" sacred unction, the right of speaking of God.
" The universe opened before me, and I learned
" that there was in man something inalienable,
" divine, eternally free—speech. The message of
" the *priest* was confided to me, and I was told to
" bear it to the ends of the world, without any one
" having the right to seal my lips a single day of
" my life. I went out of the temple with those
" grand doctrines, and I met upon the threshold
" law and bondage." Thus spoke the Abbè Lacordaire in the French Senate, when in one of his glowing bursts of oratory, he showed that the priesthood was and is the saviour not only of freedom from religious oppression, but from the tyranny of licence.

In the dawn of this freedom, it is good to remember the night of captivity. As the eighteenth century drew towards the close, the noble struggle in America for liberty infused an active spirit into the Irish Catholics, and the necessities of England at the time gained for them a hearing. In 1782 the Penal Code was relaxed, and Catholic Ireland in her gratitude sent twenty thousand brave men to the British Navy. But, hardly had the nation begun to breathe freely when the blood of '98 and the perfidy of 1800 weakened her again, and all was gloom and apathy as before. The Catholics lay prostrate, their faculties having become torpid, and their perception of pain deadened by constant suffering. A committee was formed to agitate for Catholic rights, but failed to make an impression on the Catholic body. It was at this crisis O'Connell came upon the scene. He reconstructed the Catholic Board, and his bold, earnest tones called back the Catholic spirit, but, no sooner did it begin to be active than the Viceroy of the day struck it down. It was apathy and stagnation as before. It needed a miracle to recall the Catholic spirit, and that miracle was wrought.

There had been just before this time a race of Bishops, wise men, and martyrs, who felt they should best serve the interests of their flocks by keeping *them* back from any political demonstration, and by holding *themselves* aloof from every public movement. For, thought they, a collision with the rulers would but furnish fresh opportunities to those in power to multiply the lashes that descended thick and fast, and to add to the burden which already was heavy almost beyond the power of endurance. Patience is the perfection of courage; and patient they were, and attached to their people with a devotedness without parallel in the history of any country. Thus they gained that unbounded influence over their flocks which they bequeathed to their successors.

A race of Bishops now arose, worthy of this inheritance—men to whom God gave not the spirit of fear but of power. The illustrious Dr Doyle was the leader of this heroic band. His name is mentioned because it has become a household word with us. But there were others of great account, who stood by his side all through that splendid struggle, and maintained the fight after a premature death had beaten him down. It was a stormy period from 1810 to 1829. The firm addresses of the Bishops; the courage, the energy, the majestic, earnest, irresistible logic of O'Connell; the bold, impetuous eloquence of Shiel; the enthusiasm of all classes of Irish Catholics; the *Veto* question; the Tithe question; the Forty-shilling freeholders; the Catholic Association, risen rapidly into an engine of great power; the glorious struggle for Emancipation—all bring to mind a National agitation, which furnishes the most striking instances of moral influence that are to be met with in the history of human affairs. Indeed, the more one considers that stormy period, the more he is astonished at the power of those great men, who by the mere force of personal character, were able to control the agitated tide. The more also one must admire the wisdom with which these Bishops saved the excited masses, in all their conflicts, with the ruling power, from any of those excesses that have always marked periods of popular commotion. Their attitude was at once so manly and dignified that it gained the respect and sympathy of the greatest and best men on the other side of the Channel. The highest talent in England advocated their cause. Great men, who ruled in the houses of Parliament, and great men who ruled through the public Press, wished them a hearty God-speed. "See," said they, "these men must have the rights of British "subjects." Some of them even said:—" These " fearless champions of liberty will never submit "to the yoke of Rome."

The Emancipation was won. More, however, was to be achieved for the Irish Catholics besides declaring them free to profess their religion. A hard battle was yet to be fought against the monopoly of power by those who had been taught to look on power as their birthright, and against the evils of maladministration. It will be enough to say, that in all the Catholic movements following the Emancipation Act, this spirited body of Irish Bishops were by the side of the apostle of religious freedom. O'Connell, whose great name heads so many triumphs, is himself the witness that to the influence of these Bishops were due in the greatest measure his many victories—it was through them he held in his hand the will of the nation. And, as a great leader of his Catholic fellow-countrymen, O'Connell occupied a position far above that of any man of this age—perhaps of any man of any age. With no other power but that of his eloquence, he suddenly abandons a lucrative practice at the Bar, puts himself at the head of a movement in favour of the Irish Catholics, and suddenly it swells into a great moral revolution of a whole people.

O'Connell, while he was thus the liberator of the consciences of Irish Catholics at home, took a deep interest in saving the souls of Irish Catholics abroad. From the beginning he warmly supported the establishment of a Foreign Missionary College in Dublin, and it was to him Father Hand now turned for relief. The Liberator's judgment, he knew, would guide him safely out of the feelings of keen distress which he was suffering, and his influence as Lord Mayor of Dublin was sure to obtain the Coghill Manor-House and demesne from the Corporation on favourable terms. Hence Father Hand's anxiety for a good opportunity to pour his trouble and his petition into the sympathetic ears of the Liberator. It was nearly impossible, and wholly unsatisfactory, to get hold of him during the busy hours of the day, and in the evening he retired early. The morning was incomparably the most acceptable time, but that was kept sacred to himself alone. It was commonly known that O'Connell had a most practical appreciation of the principle that early rising not only gives us more life in the same number of years, but adds likewise to the number. He was also better able to go through his serious studies in the morning when his teeming brain was clearest, and not a sound to disturb its train of thought. It was then he prepared those eloquent speeches in which his words breathed the thoughts that burned. Hence his mornings were passed in such inviolable privacy, that it was a folorn hope to attempt approaching him during that forbidden time; and upon this folorn hope Father Hand left his cell in Phibsboro' early one morning towards the end of August, 1842.

He was not long in gaining Merrion Square. In a few moments more he was passing under the windows of the well-known study, and, looking

up, he saw the blinds raised. Father Hand knew the great man was there. He knocked gently, and was answered by the faithful attendant of O'Connell. The man, moved more by pity than persuasion, consented to tell his master that there was a stranger outside in great trouble, who begged to see him for a few moments. The door of the apartment was left ajar, so that Father Hand easily overheard a dialogue to this effect:—" Did I not give you strict orders to warn off every body who might call at this hour?" " You did, your Honor; but sure he is a priest." " Oh! he is a priest, is he?" "Yes, your Honor, and he has the look of a poor priest." " Well then, show him in." There was a genial smile on O'Connell's fine Celtic face when Father Hand entered and sat down, by invitation, to recount his struggles. But, when the long story closed with the misgivings of the Irish Bishops, the Liberator was deeply moved, and spoke words of comfort, after this manner:—
" I have followed you, my dear friend, with
" an admiration, which I need not stop to
" describe. The action of the Irish Bishops
" is certainly discouraging, but quite intelligible
" as you have clearly shown. I was glad to hear
" you say that though a source of unhappiness,
" it did not make you the less hopeful. I
" heard this with pleasure, because it enables

"me as a layman to speak to you on the "subject. I now refer to it, only to sympa- "thise in the sorrow it has caused. It also "gratified me to hear of the cordial co-operation "of your own good Archbishop Murray, and above "all of the supreme sanction and blessing of the "Holy See. In these circumstances, I have no "hesitation in saying, don't relax your noble "efforts, and be assured the Irish Bishops will not "long withhold their countenance from your holy "work."

Father Hand in expressing his thanks, said he felt grateful even to emotion for this cheering reception. It banished the heavy thoughts that had been too long haunting and saddening him. He was sorry now to intrude further on the distinguished presence into which he had been so exceptionally and so kindly admitted, but he would venture to ask the Liberator's assistance in securing a suitable place for the Foreign Missionary College. There is, he added, a fine old mansion with ample grounds at Drumcondra, which the Archbishop highly commends, and being the property of the Dublin Corporation, I beg your influence as Lord Mayor to facilitate the purchase of it for the College. "Certainly," replied O'Connell. "Your cause is the cause of God, "and since it has for its special object the salva- "tion of our Catholic exiles I promise to assist "you as long as I live with my influence and my "purse."

On an early day in September, 1842, Father Hand sent in to the Dublin Corporation the following proposal:—

"To the Right Hon. the Lord Mayor, Aldermen, and Bur-
"gesses of the City of Dublin, or to the City Lease Com-
"mittee.

"My Lord and Gentlemen,

"I, the undersigned, propose to take a lease of thirty-one "years of that portion of the Corporate estate, known as Drum-"condra House, offices, demense and lands, as formerly held "under two leases by John Claudius Beresford, and lately by Sir "Guy Campbell, containing in the whole about twenty-four "Irish acres, be the same more or less, at the annual rent of "£226 16s. sterling, including receiver's fees, rent-charge "in lieu of tithe, minister's money and church cess. Said rent "to be paid half-yearly on the 29th day of September, and on "the 25th day of March in each and every year, the first pay-"ment to be made on the 25th of March next, 1843.

"I further propose to pay one year's rent in advance, the "same to be allowed to me as the rent of the 1st, 2nd, or 3rd "year after possession, should such an advance be deemed "expedient by the Corporation.

"As it is my intention to improve the property, I would be "anxious for the longest lease it is in the power of the Corpo-"ration to give.

"Since immediate residence would be to me a matter of "great consequence, I am willing to enter into possession of "the house and lands without further delay, on the good faith "of the Corporation, until they get the power of leasing the "said property to me.

"JOHN HAND."

By the influence of O'Connell as Lord Mayor these terms were accepted, and Archbishop Murray directed that the Catholic College for the Foreign Missions be opened there at once under the name of All Hallows, after its original foundation. Accordingly on the 18th of October, 1842 Father Hand went into residence with one student. On the evening of the 31st, Dr. Woodlock followed the Rev. Mr. Clarke there, and these two directors with Father Hand as superior, opened the College of All Hallows by prayer and sacrifice on the 1st November, 1842. The morning of this memorable All Saints Day, *the titular feast of the College,* these three priests offered up Mass on a small table in the oak-room of the Manor-house. In a few days after, a second student entered and with these two the regular curriculum of Ecclesiastical teaching was auspiciously begun.

But the College was a part only of Father Hand's scheme. The missionary sent out by it could not physically do more than attend to the essentials of religion. He had to visit outlying districts, which could not be reached except after many hours of weary riding in the wilderness, so that his strength and time did not leave room for any other sacred duty beyond saying Mass and administering the necessary Sacraments. Father Hand, therefore, proposed attaching to each Mission a Teaching Order of Brothers and Sisters, for the work of the schools, and the religious instruction of the old and young of both sexes. They would thus prepare the faithful to receive the Sacraments worthily; teach the children that knowledge of their holy religion which they need to practise virtue, and a fair share of secular learning, to enable them to fight the battle of life. They would also visit the sick, look after the orphans, reclaim the hardened sinners, and in one word help the priests by their holy labours, while they edified those who were neither Christians nor Catholics by their zeal, self-sacrificing charity, spotless life, and patience.

This Teaching Order of Brothers Father Hand hoped to draw from the pious youths of quick parts in our elementary schools; and he had actually arranged with the Mother Superior of the Presentation Nuns in Dublin to supply him with the Teaching Order of Sisters. This devout lady was Mrs. Carroll, to whom he often communicated the particulars of his great design, and these interesting conversations she retained in tender memory until her death a few years ago. It seemed to be her greatest happiness to recall them in the presence of anyone from All Hallows, and her tears flowed abundantly while she lamented the loss of him, who possessed the masterful grasp of mind to devise, and the strength of will to undertake such a noble plan of keeping alive the Faith in every corner of the English-speaking world.

It was, first of all, for the scattered children of his own race and creed—the Catholic emigrants of the dear old country—Father Hand framed his holy scheme. There were in his day Irish Catholics forced to emigrate from sheer want of the necessaries of life, and some who left to seek their fortune. These were the first objects of his solicitude, and surely there could be none more worthy of his sympathy and sacrifice. Imagine a young Irish girl, fresh from the innocence of her Catholic home, on board the vessel which bears her across the great deep, to make a living among the strangers. The most stringent rules of the ship are ineffectual for her protection, unless the priest is there.

Then, after passing unscathed through this ordeal, there are on shore wicked persons watching to make her defencelessness a source of profit. The late Mr. Maguire, in his admirable book on the Irish in America, tells the story of a Catholic girl from Ireland, who, on arriving in one of the cities of the United States, took service unsuspectingly from a person of infamous character, and was hurried off through the streets to her terrible fate. An old Irishwoman happened to see her passing, and, moved with pity, she rushed upon the enemy, and literally tore the victim from his grasp. Thus, by the merest accident, this innocent young creature was saved. With the priest by her side, on landing she is always safe; but in his absence many like her have been brought to ruin. There is hardly one who has not read or heard of the allurements offered to pure-minded emigrant girls on board ship, or immediately on landing. What would not their good fathers and mothers in the old country give to have them under the care of one of Father Hand's missionaries? True, the danger is not so formidable as it was; still it exists, and under our eyes. Father Hand wished sincerely that the sons and daughters of poor Ireland would remain on the soil where they were born, for he deeply cherished the love of home in opposition to the spirit of emigration. But our starving people, flying from these shores for food and shelter, moved him to establish his Foreign Missionary College; and, now that this emigration is going on, though happily in diminished numbers, it is certain that the salvation of hundreds, even thousands of our young and inexperienced poor Catholics, will be placed in peril by its stream, unless the missionary accompany them.

Then, there is the danger of sickness, which renders the presence of the priest on board ship imperatively necessary. Imagine this typical young Irish Catholic girl stricken down on the passage by a fatal illness, and crying for a priest to absolve her before death. What would not Father Hand have done to keep one of his missionaries within reach of that poor soul, burning with the faith of the old country, and the early memories of her mother's piety, to pronounce the words of peace and reconciliation. The consequences of serious illness on board ship are not so direful as when the emigration from this country was carried on in sailing vessels, with a passage of six or eight weeks' duration, and when the foulness of the lower decks, acting upon the starved condition of their living freight, produced pestilence. This was in the famine of 1846 and 1847, when 10,000 Irish Catholic emigrants filled the fever-sheds of Montreal and Quebec. One Sunday morning during the black days of this famine, an emigrant vessel, driven by stress of weather, put into the nearest harbour. The plague had already broken out on board, and the priest of the place was called from the altar after Mass. As soon as he arrived on deck his ears were struck with shrieks of agony from the dark hold below. Hurrying down through the poisonous atmosphere, to a fine young man writhing on a rude bed, there was barely time to shrive him when the fever got into his brain. The poor fellow became delirious, and was dead when the priest came back from attending a mother and daughter who were dying in another corner, and raving of home and kind friends.

Though the occasion of these terrible scenes has passed, not to return, with God's mercy, the danger of sickness and contagious disease in the emigrant ship always exists. Therefore, either the missionary must be on the spot, or the spiritual wants of our poor Catholic emigrants will be neglected. And it is precisely on board ship the missionary is able to prepare Irish Catholic exiles, by good moral instructions and the Sacraments, for the temptations that await them among the strangers. There is no better proof of this than that furnished by one of the missionaries from All Hallows in 1851. That year Rev. Mr. Woods, in going to his mission in Van Diemen's Land, as it was then called, got charge of the convicts to be transported from Ireland to Hobart Town. As soon as he joined the ship, penitents flocked to him to hear their confessions, in order that they might be prepared to encounter the perils of the voyage. It was a duty he gladly accepted, and in a few days before they weighed anchor at Queenstown he admitted over 200 of the convicts to Holy Communion!

But to meet the spiritual necessities of our Catholic emigrants, it is not enough for the Missionary to be on board the ship and present at their landing. He must be with them until they are actually settled in their new homes, near a priest and an altar like what they left behind. Up to this moment All Hallows has not been able to *accompany*, but merely to *follow* our Catholic emigrants, and even in the matter of *following* them much remains to be accomplished. An All Hallows Missionary, writing so late as last October, from *Mercedes, Buenos Ayres,* sent to his *Alma Mater* the following message for help:—

"What was held up in the late appeal for the College as a "sad state of affairs in the Banda Oriental—a countryman "dying without the last Sacraments and unable to confess in "the language he understood—may shortly become a more sad "and frequent reality in the Argentine Republic. There the "Irish are comparatively very few; here I should say we number "not much short of 20,000. Other estimates place the number "much higher. To attend that number, scattered over a vast "extent of territory, there are only six chaplains, with two more "discharging other duties. Some few years ago there was "double the number of chaplains, although the English-speaking "population was certainly not greater. At present I have to "attend, once a month each four different churches, distant "from fifty to one hundred miles from where I reside; also "the sick calls. In each place there is a large attendance. I "am not the only one so situated. I need not say there are "plenty of priests in the country who discharge parochial and "other duties, who speak and administer in the language of "the country—Spanish. Scarcely any of them speak English, "nor are they supposed to. The Irish speak English—most "of them nothing else—and rarely confess in any other "language—some from inclination, but most from necessity; "and I believe on the whole they are as attentive to their "religious duties as their countrymen at home or elsewhere."

Much, therefore, is yet to be done in order to complete the work which Father Hand, under the divine inspiration, marked out for his missionaries, and which with God's blessing will not be left unfinished. The same charity which has enabled his Institution to do so much, will stimulate and strengthen it to do more. Thus the tender invitation which has been sent last summer by the Catholic Bishops of the young and vigorous Church in the United States, to their brethren of the older and more venerable Church of Ireland, will be happily accepted, and effectual measures adopted for further securing the spiritual as well as temporal interests of the Irish Catholic emigrant.

Another class of the most spiritually destitute among the scattered children of our country are Catholic Irishmen serving in the British army and navy. This is prominently set forth in one of the earliest reports of All Hallows, and in the annals of the same College for 1860, the statement is emphasized by an affecting letter from a Catholic officer, quartered with his regiment in the Island of St. Helena:—" Had you but seen," he writes, " as I have, the awful and mysterious struggle of " the dying Catholic soldier—if you were but to " hear his wild cry of anguish for the priest of his " loved and cherished religion—and could you but " witness his last look of agonised despair, as his " troubled spirit was about to take its departure " from the frail tenement of clay, unsolaced by " those sacred rites of the Holy Church, which " bring such comfort and consolation to the dying " sinner, you would, I am sure, agree with me, " that no sacrifice would be too great to prevent

"the recurrence of so heart-rending a scene as I
"have feebly attempted to sketch, of the death-
"bed, not of one, but unfortunately of many of my
"poor fellow-Catholic soldiers."

This is a true account of the sore spiritual need that surrounds the Irish Catholics serving in the British army and navy, and when we remember how much they have to endure; their hardships and their risks, it is clearly the duty of Father Hand's Missionaries to minister to them. True, the State is bound to provide for the eternal interests of these brave men, seeing that they give their lives in defence of the country, and the least they can get in return is to be afforded the means of practising their holy religion. Irish Catholic soldiers and sailors are sustaining England on sea and land, therefore it would be a cruel wrong for the Government of this great Empire not to send priests to prepare them for death in the unhealthy atmosphere of military stations in foreign service, and on the eve of battle. Not only is the Government obliged by duty to make this religious provision, but in doing so it confers a great benefit on the country. Catholic soldiers and sailors, yielding to the weakness of human nature, grow cold from time to time in their religious duties. But when war has been declared, and they are ordered to the front their practical faith invariably revives, and it is only after having made their peace with God that they face the danger with intrepidity.

The Government of England does employ the services of the priest for the Catholics in the British Army and Navy, but not in sufficient supply, and a Protestant Government cannot well understand why Catholic soldiers and sailors require a larger number of chaplains in proportion than Protestants. But Catholics, in the discharge of their religious duties, must draw much more liberally on the ministrations of the priest than Protestants are bound to do on the spiritual offices of the parson. Hearing confessions alone of England's Catholic soldiers and sailors is sufficient to occupy the whole time of more than double, perhaps treble, the number of military chaplains assigned to them. This was well shown in the Egyptian Campaign of 1882. In the British force sent out from England on that occasion, the Irish element was considerable, and everyone remembers that the 18th Royal Irish and the Royal Irish Fusiliers were among the first in the brilliant attack on Tel-el-Kebir. Now, nearly all the Irish Catholic soldiers then in Egypt were making their confessions for some days before going into action. Out of 700 Catholics in one corps alone, there were only thirty who had not prepared themselves for death; and thus they kept the hands full, not only of their own chaplains, but of several priests from the Order of St. Francis at Alexandria. Were it not for their assistance, the Catholic chaplains would not have been able to attend to the spiritual wants of those under their care. These good Franciscan Fathers were, no doubt, kind and charitable in giving them their help, but it may be presumed they were foreigners. It is, however, well known that Irish Catholics prefer the priests of their own nationality, who are acquainted with their habits and manners, and consequently, in the present instance, the Irish missionary ought to be present with their brave countrymen, to break to them the Bread of Life, or co-operate with their chaplains in doing so. Therefore, the scattered Irish Catholics, for whom Father Hand formed his comprehensive scheme, are still in a state of severe spiritual destitution; and this can remain unrelieved only for a time under the force of pressing circumstances—until the claim of the Irish Catholic emigrant and Irish Catholic soldier and sailor shall call more loudly for sympathy and generous sacrifice.

CHAPTER XI.

" THEY THAT SOW IN TEARS SHALL REAP IN JOY."

CONTENTS.—Circular announcing the opening of All Hallows—The urgent messages that came to Father Hand from Bishops in India, America, Australia, Scotland, and North Wales—Father Hand's grief at not being able, through poverty, to send priests to destitute Missions—His programme of devotions for a nine-days' public supplication to God that He send a supply for these pressing wants—His patient endurance in collecting charitable donations from the Catholics of Dublin and Meath—He is still a prominent figure in the recollection of the old inhabitants where he passed—His long journeys and perilous adventures when overtaken by a storm—His coming home late, and praying long in his wet clothes before the Blessed Sacrament, while his faithful servant, Pat Daly, kept anxious watch—How he disarmed prejudice by an humble sense of his own excellent abilities—His encouraging reports to the Cardinal Prefect of Propaganda—He turned a part of the old Building at All Hallows into a College Chapel, which he opened to the public, and where he catechised the poor children of the country round—How the old and young of the neighbourhood blessed him for the wonderful change he had wrought in their midst—How his Foreign Missionary College was extending its bounds.

THE opening of All Hallows was announced by public circular, with this heading:—"*Catholic College at Dublin for the Foreign Missions, expressly sanctioned by His Holiness Pope Gregory XVI., under the special protection of the Sacred Congregation of Propaganda at Rome, and the*

immediate patronage of His Grace the Most Rev. Dr. Murray, Archbishop of Dublin." It sets forth, with the spirit and conscientiousness of Father Hand, the object of the Institution and its claim for support:—" A number of Clergymen, considering the
" lamentable want of Catholic Missionaries in the
" Colonies, America and other foreign countries,
" seeing also that there are in Ireland hundreds of
" highly qualified young men, who would most
" willingly consecrate themselves to the laborious,
" but consoling duties of the Foreign Missions,
" were a College founded to educate them for that
" purpose, and knowing, moreover, the desire of
" the faithful to contribute towards so holy a work,
" have resolved to live in community, and devote
" themselves gratuitously to the establishment and
" direction of such a College at Dublin, as the most
" effectual means of supplying those vast regions
" with Apostolic Missionaries.

" The commencement of such a work is always
" the most difficult ; but now that the plan of this
" College, so much wanted and so long desired,
" has been sufficiently matured, and fully approved
" of, it is confidently hoped that all Catholics will
" be prompt and generous in contributing towards
" its immediate establishment. They cannot sub-
" scribe to a work better calculated to promote the
" glory of God, to extend the kingdom of Christ,
" and to secure the salvation of souls."

In a short time urgent messages for help were coming from destitute missions to the College. The Bishops from these missions sent to Father Hand facts of the most saddening description:—" I " look to your establishment under God," writes Dr. Fennelly of Madras, " for the stability of our Mis-" sion. It is a disheartening reflection that we are " not numerous enough to break the Bread of Life " to the children of the household, much less to " gather in the heathen .... The poor " people here are daily crying out for no less a " number than eight priests. The natives have " hitherto been considerably neglected in our " Mission, partly because the priests who have " been arriving of late in this country, are ignorant " of the native language, and partly owing to the " absolute want of Missionaries. We have upwards " of 90,000 Catholics—some say 100,000—in the " Vicariate, and for all these we have only twenty " priests, who, with some exceptions, are not yet " able to speak in Hindoostanee. No wonder, " then, that we look forward with intense anxiety " to your College at Drumcondra. It is the hope " of India and of the British Colonies." Then there were Bishops from America, from Australia, each repeating the same sorrowful story. Catholic parents without a priest to bless their union, to baptize their children, to hear their confessions, to prepare them for death. Dr. Polding, Archbishop

of Sydney, New South Wales, Australia, assured Father Hand that:—"In every part of this im-
"mense territory, there are hundreds and hundreds
"belonging to our holy religion, who can never
"hear Mass, who must live and die without the
"Sacraments. My heart bleeds when I think of
"their miserable state—the famine of their souls.
"I shall rely upon your kind sympathy in our
"wants to procure for us priests, such as God loves,
"and man respects, rejoicing to suffer if such be
"the will of their Divine Master."

Dr. Hynes of Demerara implored aid in these few harrowing words:—"I am deplorably in want
"of priests—good and holy ones. The number
"of Missionaries in my Vicariate will be soon
"reduced to *three;*" while Dr. Byrne, Bishop of Little Rock, Arkansas, accompanied his petition by this mournful account:—"I should be glad to
"know if you have two or three young men of
"piety and talent, who may have their studies
"nearly finished. I have an extensive diocese,
"and have found in many parts of it Catholic
"families, who had no opportunity of seeing a
"priest for *twenty-five or thirty years.* I spent last
"Easter Sunday on the banks of the Red River,
"opposite Texas, instructing children for Baptism
"from the age of five to seventeen. In one county
"alone of this large state, I have lately met sixty
"families whose parents or grandparents were

"Irish, and had fallen away from the faith, for the want of a Ministry and are now attached to anything or everything the most fashionable. At another time I shall give you some details of my Mission in search of the strayed and the fallen."

And the Bishop of Dubuque, Iowa, began his letter thus:—"I take the liberty of writing to you in order to obtain as soon as practicable a young Missionary from your excellent institution. My diocese is poor; I have only a few priests, and the Missions are severe. We have to visit wild Indians in a harsh climate. In a word, we stand in need of truly devoted priests."

But the cry, uttered nearer home, was still more piercing. It was wafted to Father Hand from Scotland by Dr. Gillis, Bishop of Edinburgh:—"We have thousands of your fellow-countrymen at this moment in the most hopeless state of spiritual destitution. The most favourable opportunities of forming new Missions are every day slipping away from us, and the violent Protestant papers are actually sneering at us for not providing our various Missions with clergymen, and exulting *over the fall of Rome*. For God's sake, if you know of any such priests as above described, send me one or two."

From Glasgow Dr. Scott mentioned his wants in a more plaintive tone:—"This Mission is entirely a new creation, for it is only thirty-six "years since I was the only Catholic Missionary in all the counties which form the Lowland part of this Vicariate, where at present there are twenty priests, and where many more would be required. Our flocks are almost entirely made up of poor Irish, who, from various causes, were forced to expatriate themselves in a state of abject poverty. Of course it cannot be supposed that they are able to do much. From the failure of trade, and from a new kind of epidemic fever, by which almost all our poor labouring people were attacked in our manufacturing towns last year, our flocks are reduced to a very great degree of poverty; and had it not been for the very liberal allocation granted to us last year by the Society for the Propagation of the Faith, some of our chapels would have been exposed to the danger of being sold."

Dr. Brown, who ruled the extensive diocese of North Wales, congratulated Father Hand on having established All Hallows, and begged him to admit a few Welsh boys, since one of the most effective means in the hands of the Missionary to bring back the Principality of Wales to the Catholic Church, is a fluency in speaking the Welsh language:—"I express imperfectly my sentiments when I say that I am thankful to Almighty God, and, after Him, to yourself and zealous co-operators, for that important work of

"Catholic charity, which is being so auspiciously carried into effect—the Catholic Missionary College of All Hallows. May it be crowned with the fulness of all spiritual and temporal blessings. The one great difficulty in the way here is fluency in the Welsh tongue, which appears to many sensible men, as it does decidedly to me, of the utmost importance to the conversion of the natives of the Principality. Except on the coast, there are few of the lower class who understand English, and those who do are mostly so wedded to their native tongue, that they will refuse attention to religious truths delivered in any other. Had this national prejudice been duly indulged a few years since—before the Baptists and Methodists deluged the land with their preachers in the Welsh language—I have reason to believe that the Welsh, who never welcomed the Established doctrines, but retained their anxious attachment for the religion which their fathers had professed, would be at this day emulators of the believing Irish nation. . . .
"If I might be permitted to send one or two Welsh boys to your college, on low pensions, as my means would permit, a great service might be rendered me. Your plan of education and discipline meets fully my approval."

All Hallows had no Missionaries to send to these thousands of our own kith and kin, yearning with the most intense desire for the saving ministrations of their holy religion; and there was but slender hopes of its being able to afford them relief even in the near future. The money collected every day was barely sufficient to furnish the necessaries of life to the limited number of students in residence, and therefore, the idea of making provision for more candidates, could not be entertained. Father Hand was overwhelmed with grief, and to add to his affliction, he encountered, in quarters where he went for encouragement, bitter taunts, cruel insinuations on the vanity, no less than rashness, of having undertaken an enterprise which demanded a higher order of abilities than he possessed. His heart was literally breaking, and in the deepest distress he invited all in the College to join in a public and fervent supplication to God that He send a supply for the pressing wants of the Foreign Missions. He wrote out a programme of devotion for the purpose, and surrounded by his students and colleagues, he carried out this faithfully for nine consecutive days. It is to this effect :—

"You shall ask whatever you will, and it shall be done unto you."—John xv. 7.

"Novena to the Blessed Virgin and our Guardian Angels, "that through their intercession Almighty God may direct our "counsels, and help us to secure the temporal concerns of this "Institution, in a permanent manner, for His own greater glory, "and the salvation of souls.

"From next Saturday morning till the Monday week following, we shall 1st, on awakening offer to the Immaculate Heart of the Mother of God, our *thoughts, affections, words,* and *actions* of the day, praying that she may unite all these with her own, and thus present them to the loving Heart of her Divine Son, Jesus.

"2. By diligence, recollection and purity of intention during the day, we shall endeavour to render our *thoughts, affections, words and actions* worthy of being thus offered to the Sacred Heart of Jesus, through the Immaculate Heart of Mary. Let us also during the day at the beginning of Mass, of Study and going into Class, think for an instant of the pure thoughts and rapturous affections of the Heart of Mary, and try to emulate them, ever so little.

"3. We shall recite the Rosary with particular devotion, and during it as well as at Mass let us recommend the wants of the College to the Sacred Hearts of Jesus and Mary. The *Ave Maris Stella* shall be sung after Mass, and a prayer offered up to our Guardian Angels, which prayer can be repeated at our visits to the Blessed Sacrament.

"4. We shall observe more than usual recollection these days, and at breakfast and supper let there be *five* minutes spiritual conversation.

"5. It is suggested that each Director say as many Masses as his devotion may dictate for the object of this Novena, and perform some little act of mortification, and let all this be for the greater glory of God, the honour of the Blessed Virgin Mary, and our Guardian Angels.

"J. M. J."

In this straitened situation of affairs, Father Hand's fortitude was truly admirable, especially in the patience and endurance with which he begged from door to door in Dublin during the day. At evening he hastened home to meet the students in Chapel, and though tired with toil and fasting, he was sure to be there. As Superior, he had to give them spiritual lecture, which he regarded as of such indispensable necessity, that it was never omitted, unless his waiting on the charitable Catholics of Meath, or of some distant parts of the County Dublin, kept him back unavoidably.

And he is still a prominent figure in the recollection of the old inhabitants where he made these long journeys. They remember him, muffled in a threadbare cloak, which, with a worn-out umbrella, he carried about with him till his death. He always travelled in a gig, terribly out of repair, and drawn by a pony, which tradition endows with wonderful sagacity.

Under these circumstances many a perilous adventure he had, which has been told in substance by one living near the College, who though young then, knew well how to love Father Hand, and to watch his wonderful labours with tender solicitude. This man has since prospered in the world, and from the savings of his honest industry has given so liberally to the support of All Hallows that his name is there engraved on enduring marble among its munificent benefactors. It may be interesting to add that he has also presented the College recently with a precious relic of Father Hand—the small table on which he said Mass in the old Manor-house during the short interval before an altar had been raised within. He has described Father Hand's privations on some of these long journeys to be after this manner :— Whenever any duty awaited Father Hand at the College, neither gentle pressure of kind friends, nor the fury of the elements could keep him from returning home. Though a storm having sprung up in the evening, should become more violent every moment, the well-known pony was brought round to the door, and struck out into a bold rapid trot as soon as the priest mounted the gig. The wind, however, on some of these occasions proved too many, for he had not gone far when the fierce gusts brought the pony to a dead stand. Then, after considerable delay, he was again making slow progress until the driving rain lashed himself and the pony with such fury that it was necessary to withdraw into a shelter. But the thick darkness and the roar of the tempest had no terror for Father Hand, who sat through all in quiet unconcern behind his brave little steed. Animated by a certain religious enthusiasm, he did not heed the alarming incidents of the road, and pushed forward on his difficult path.

Father Hand did not get back to All Hallows until its laborious students were all asleep in the mantle of deep sleep that covers all human thoughts. The lights had been put out, but one of the domestic staff kept anxious watch. Pat Daly was so sincerely attached to Father Hand that he claimed the privilege of sitting up for him. He was a favourite with the other servants, whom he gathered round a good fire on these occasions, and talked away in his best vein till they dropped off one by one. Pat, however, kept his post like a trusted sentinel, though it was the kind of night one would appreciate a comfortable bed. At last he heard his name called through the window. In a moment the front door was opened, and Father Hand entered—his face stained with the drippings of the rain which had soaked into his hat. "Pat, my son," said he, in a voice trembling from the long exposure, "just warm a few potatoes for my dinner; fetch them with cold meat into the dining-room, and when you are ready come for me to the chapel." Pat shuddered at the thought of the priest going to the chapel in his damp clothes. "Oh! your Reverence, I am sorry to see you so bad with the wet. It is strange, to say the least, that you should venture out on a night, when every one ought to thank God for the shelter of a house. Won't you come to the fire for a while and warm yourself." The priest interrupted him: "Pat," said he, "do what I have told you; and mind don't make any noise for I wish to slip off to my room after a little as quietly as possible." The servant stood aghast at the command; but recovering himself in a moment, he promised prompt obedience, for there was that in the priest's tone, which was to him a sure indication that remonstrance was useless.

Father Hand divested himself of his cloak and having consigned it to the servant, retired into the chapel. He was not long there when the summons to dinner followed him, for Pat in his great concern about his master's health, did not take much time to prepare the modest meal. But Father Hand was not coming, and when Pat went back again to call him, he was struck with awe to find the holy man in rapt contemplation before the Blessed Sacrament. After a lengthened suspense, Pat, stealing towards him, whispered into his ear that it was late bedtime, and he could sit up no longer. "God bless you, my son," answered the priest, "I am sorry to have kept you till this hour from your well-earned rest;" and, rising from his knees, he made his way slowly after Pat into the dining-room. There the faithful attendant took his leave in a few minutes, and in doing so seized the hand extended to bless him in both his, and kissed it with passionate reverence.

Father Hand being thus left to himself, fell immediately into a train of deep thought about the great work in which he was engaged. Then it was that in the solemn silence the difficulties with which he was encompassed, started up like so many spectres, and filled him with terror. In the dismal moaning of the wind outside he was again listening to the lamentations that came to him from so many Bishops, and he fancied he heard with painful distinctness their voices beseeching him:— "Oh! for God's sake, send us Missionaries." Under the feelings excited by this imagination, he fairly broke down and wept when he thought of his poverty. With his tears he watered the morsel of cold meat and few toasted potatoes before him; and though the day was one of unusual fatigue, he sank upon his knees, and remained far into the night praying fervently for help and consolation. Next morning, at 6.30, he was first in the College Chapel for meditation with the students—a rule which he kept with the utmost exactness.

Father Hand is also remembered in the localities he frequented as possessing remarkable winning powers, and exercising them invariably with infallible success. It appears his great anxiety just now was to stand well with the Dublin clergy, that he might have their good will and good word. This he often mentioned in confidence to one of them, a true friend, who, at present full of years and merit, occupies a high place among the dignataries of the Venerable Chapter of Dublin. This devoted priest often cheered Father Hand in his trials at this time; and, happening to meet him one day in town, said:—"By the way, I am entertaining a large circle of College friends and other members of the parochial clergy this evening. Now, you ought to come, and make an impression on them." Father Hand, grateful beyond expression for this thoughtful attention, accepted the invitation, not to dinner, because it would interfere with him in his work, but to join them later on. Accordingly, when he arrived, the host exclaimed, in a voice to arrest attention:—"Oh, this is my friend Father Hand; I must show him hospitality." The remark was received with a noisy murmour of censure, which showed unmistakably that Father Hand was to them an unwelcome visitor. It is probable that most of them did not know him personally, and perhaps did not care to know him, for, doubtless, they heard enough to make them not regard him with confidence and respect. They may have believed, as some others did at the time, that he was rash without skill, so that, yielding to this dangerous impulse of his nature, he built a castle in the air, and was vexing and worrying every one for money to sustain him in it. This estimate of Father Hand, and the information on which it was founded, were entirely fallacious. The host, therefore, anxious to convince his guests of this, asked them to receive Father Hand for an hour or so, as he was sure not to stay long from the pressing work to which God had called him. There was no objection to this proposal, coming as it did from one who made them all so happy at his own board, and the unwelcome visitor was brought into the room.

Father Hand, on entering, met with a warm and genial reception from the host, who introduced him to those present. The recollections of College days and incidents of the Ministry circulated freely round the board, and Father Hand joined with much relish, laughing and talking away, for no one enjoyed more heartily a lively or amusing anecdote, and no one knew better how to relieve the mind by the interchange of pleasant discourse. True, he maintained a studied reserve with the outside world in his conversation—a gravity in his deportment; but with his colleagues in time of recreation, and indeed with all whom he met in hospitable society, he relaxed even to facetiousness. To see him, therefore, on this occasion, and hear him so mirthful, was an agreeable but astonishing spectacle to those who expected to find him dull and austere. They began to feel now that the man was misrepresented or badly interpreted, and they liked him the more on that account. The host, who was closely observing them, perceived at once that their prejudice had been disarmed, as he anticipated, and with nice judgment he turned the conversation into the channel of All Hallows. Father Hand seized the opportunity, and nothing could be more captivating than the picture he drew of the wants of the Foreign Missions. There was no heart there that was not touched by it, for when Father Hand rose to leave, all stood up, wishing his noble work success, and begging him to put down their names on the list of his annual subscribers.

Now, what was it that acted like a spell on this company? It was not certainly persuasive eloquence, for he had it not. No; it came from the simple language of an humble, earnest priest, and his unostentatious worth. From a sense of humility, or the vanity of human things, Father Hand hid out of the public view his natural gifts and solid learning; and this intuitive dislike for display came to be regarded as the mark of a mind of inferior calibre. But, in close relations with him, one saw that his mind was cast in a superior mould, though he tried to conceal it behind a charming modesty. Herein lay the secret of the spell which he exercised on this and similar occasions.

In his passage through the painful ordeal of this period, Father Hand never repined, hesitated or relaxed, but day after day he was off on the same weary mission, and even sent an encouraging report of his progress to the Cardinal Prefect of Propaganda at Rome :—

"MOST EMINENT PRINCE,

"It is now some two years since Your Eminence and the "Sacred Congregation graciously approved the project of "establishing in Dublin a College for the Foreign Missions, "especially within English territory. The condescension then "shown by Your Eminence and the Sacred Congregation, "makes me hope it will gratify you to hear what we have been "doing . . . .

"Though this house and land were secured for many months "previously, the College was not opened till last November. "The number of Students, which was necessarily small in the "beginning, has since increased to thirty-eight, and they are "destined for the following Missions, viz.:—Four for Vincennes; "one for New York in the United States ; three for British "Guiana ; three for Trinidad ; two for Calcutta (India) ; one "for Agra (India); seven for Madras (India) ; one for the "Cape of Good Hope (Africa); two for New South Wales "(Australia), and six for Scotland, etc.

"The Bishops of these several dioceses have promised to "give £10 a year towards the maintenance of each of their "subjects, and the Students themselves contribute an equal "sum, while the balance, required for their support, is supplied "by generous alms, which, I am confident, will soon place this "College on a permanent basis.

"It is cheering to see so many candidates presenting them- "selves. This fact shows what an abundant supply of zealous "priests the faith and piety of Catholic Ireland could yield for "the Foreign Missions, if this College were not hampered by "poverty.

"Already a great deal has been done, but much remains to be "accomplished. So far, we are only four priests to superintend "the general working of the Institution, and teach Dogmatic "and Moral Theology, Philosophy, etc. We expect, however, "an accession to our number very soon, and we have, with the "approbation of His Grace the Archbishop of Dublin, formed "ourselves into a community of secular priests, devoted gratuitously, and without vows, to the education of Missionaries for places abroad.

"Although our titular feast is *All Saints*, we are anxious to have the College placed under the special protection of the Most Holy Virgin Mary, Immaculately Conceived, and the patronage of St. Francis Xavier, Apostle of the Indies. We, therefore, humbly ask Your Eminence to obtain for us the privilege of celebrating the feast of the Immaculate Conception of Our Blessed Lady as a double of the first class, and that of St. Francis Xavier, as a double of the second class. By this we hope to foster in our own hearts and in those of the Students, a tender devotion to the ever Blessed Virgin, Queen of the Apostles, and to the Great Apostle of the Indies, who did so much for the Foreign Missions.

"In conclusion, we beg to renew the expressions of our humble gratitude for the favours which Your Eminence has already conferred on us. And, now joined by the members of this Community in kissing the sacred purple, and in offering our respectful homage to Your Eminence, and the other Cardinals of the Sacred Congregation of Propaganda.

"I have the honor to remain,
"Your Eminence's most obedient, devoted, and humble servant,
"JOHN HAND.
"All Hallows, 7th October, 1843."

The hopes expressed by Father Hand in this report were not long delayed. Donations and subscriptions had swelled to such encouraging proportions in his hands, that he was now able to spare a sufficient sum for turning one of the old buildings on the premises into a study-hall, and the loft over it into a dormitory. This temporary accommodation, together with a plain wing, added to the Manor-house, gave ample room for the

numerous candidates, who kept loudly knocking at his door, and who at the call of God came in such force that the one present on the opening day, increased to fify-four. Thus in one year from the date of his first report, Father Hand could write to the Cardinal Prefect of Propaganda: —" When I had last year the honour of report-
"ing to Your Eminecne, this College had thirty-
" eight students, taught and superintended by four
" priests. Since then the thirty-eight students
" have increased to fifty-four, and I have the
" happiness of being surrounded at present by
" eight zealous priests, associated with me in this
" undertaking."

This growth in the number of his Directors and students continued to advance steadily, and on the 29th of December, 1845, about five months before his lamented death, he made the following return to Cardinal Fransoni, Prefect of the Propaganda: —"When addressing Your Eminence this time last
" year, the number of our students was fifty-four,
" and that of our Directors eight. At present there
" are sixty-five students in the College, and some
" twenty more have been sent to their respective
" Bishops, to finish their course near the scene of
" their future labours. Thirty-three of the students
" in residence are reading a graduated course
" of Dogmatic and Moral Theology, Sacred Scrip-
" ture and Ecclesiastical history. There are

"eight in Mental Philosophy, with which they
" combine a course of Physical Science, and
" Mathematics. The Rhetoric class has nine, etc.
" and all are instructed in the Gregorian Chant,
" Sacred Eloquence, with some of the modern
" languages. Thank God, the charity of the faith-
" ful, especially here in Ireland, is contributing a
" large-handed support to the College. Up to this
" time £7,500, have been received, while the
" expenses did not exceed £5,000. We have also
" made provision for a refectory, additional dormi-
" tories, and study-hall, but with all these expenses
" during the last three years, there is still to the good
" a sum of £2,500, or about 11,500 Roman crowns."

A part of the old buildings, which had not been touched by the recent improvements, Father Hand converted about this time into the College Chapel, which, with the Archbishop's leave, he opened to the public on all Sundays and holidays of obligation. Here the Missionary work, he loved so much at Phibsboro', was revived. Every Saturday he attended in the confessional, and on Sundays the time that he could be spared from College duties was devoted by him to the instruction in the catechism of the poor children who flocked from the country round. There are many, not yet old in this neighbourhood, who remember what this place was then. They marked how new buildings rose up in connection with the old Manor-house; they saw a roof spreading over them from side to side, and a large cross of stone, set in front. Old men blessed God for the beautiful College that was erected to His honour on the site, as they had been told, of All Hallows stately Priory, where once the monks were to be heard morning and evening, through the aisles of the church, singing matins or vespers in the choir under the great east window. The young also came to have a veneration for the new establishment, that stood above their historic little village, and they blessed what their fathers blessed. A day came round on which it was given out that a chapel which the public would be allowed to enter, had been constructed within, and they remember well how the news filled their hearts with joy. They do not forget the earnest fervour with which they assisted there at the adorable Sacrifice of the Mass, and how when it was over they went home, blessing God together. They now came regularly to the sacred mysteries, and they saw a wonderful change. Rich soil, such as on the banks of the lazy Tolka below, gathered upon those parts, which were choked with stones and the rankest weeds. The ruggedness and deformities disappeared, leaving nothing now but level plain and gentle slope—a delicious carpet, soft-looking as a palace park. The gaps in the great wall round about were filled up, and in the summer the venerable trees within, put on their leaves, and people passing in and out on the Sunday looked at them as though they had never looked on trees or leaves before. Now, who brought about this change? It looked like enchantment, but who exercised the spell? They knew the holy man, and they loved him. This was Father Hand, who counted every stone, and measured every beam in the erection and repairs then effected in the buildings, and carefully inspected every improvement made in the grounds. Thus, day after day Father Hand's College for the Foreign Missions was extending its bounds and putting on new beauties. The difficulties that threatened its infancy were disappearing, and in less than four years it was thronged with students, taught and directed by a staff of able and devoted men, who have left their mark not only on the history of All Hallows, but on that of the whole Irish Church. In this comparatively short interval Father Hand sent out several Missionaries, and in the flattering testimonies of their zeal which were coming to him, he began to reap in joy the seed he sowed in tears.

CHAPTER XII.

HE DIED FULL OF LABOURS, BUT NOT FULL OF DAYS.

CONTENTS.—Father Hand sacrificed himself to the great purpose of his life—He contracted a complaint which his exhausted system was not able to overcome—In April, 1846, he was prostrated by an acute attack of hæmorrhage from the lungs, which rendered his recovery hopeless—Archbishop Murray's message of condolence at the sad news—How Father Hand spent his last days on earth—His farewell address to the Directors—Affecting scene at his death, which happened on the 20th of May, 1846—The Directors, Students, and poor children of the neighbourhood sobbing around the coffin at his funeral—His grave is under the shadow of a ruin in the College grounds, and marked only by a simple wooden cross—No higher tribute can be paid to his memory than to pour out one's soul by that precious earth, which covers his resting-place—The two most prominent features in the character of Father Hand were a stern devotion to what he believed to be the call of God, and an abiding spirit of labour—How effectively he was helped by confidence in God—His simple candour, and kind-hearted geniality gained him the favour of every one who had to do with him—By his indefatigable zeal in the propagation of the Faith he imparted vigour to its purpose—It is a melancholy reflection that a career so full of usefulness to mankind, and glory to God should have been thus early arrested—His mission though short has been the seed-time of a rich harvest—Those who have succeeded him pray that they may water well what he planted, so that God may give the increase.

THE privations endured by Father Hand in begging for the College, as described in the last chapter, soon began to tell on a constitution that was never strong. But instead of slackening his endeavours, he seemed to apply himself to it more vigorously. He allowed no consideration of health to excuse him. He went about as before; for work—active, energetic, self-sacrificing work—seemed a law of his being, and "in all his works he gave thanks to the Holy One, and to the Most High, with words of glory." The higher he ascended the mountain, the firmer were his steps. One should see him in the early morning pushing his way along the desolate road, and crossing heights, against wind and rain to appreciate his active zeal. Many is the time this sight could be witnessed. To the material eye, indeed, he would appear borne along on his tottering gig, but, if the veil were lifted, one might see him carried on Angels' wings. And the late evenings he continued the same practice of coming home in the roar of the tempest, paying long visits to the Blessed Sacrament in wet clothes, watering with his tears the morsel of cold meat and few potatoes, and robbing himself of his necessary sleep by remaining to commune with God, long after his faithful servant had ceased to watch. Thus did he persevere until the body's frame was worn, and an abscess had formed on one of his lungs. By sacrificing himself after this manner to the great purpose of his life, he contracted a complaint which his exhausted system was not able to overcome, and had a fatal ending.

While the disease, thus contracted, was slowly but surely consuming him, he encountered the biting winds of March, 1846, in raising funds for the College through the County Meath, and came home on Thursday (April 2nd), to die. The following Sunday and Monday, which happened that year to fall in Holy Week, he struggled to say Mass in his sick-room. It was this effort, perhaps, that induced an acute attack of hæmorrhage from the lungs, which prostrated him. From this moment his body drooped, but his mind was clear as usual, and busy in making acts of resignation to the Divine will. It was truly affecting to hear him in melting accents thanking God for His many mercies to himself, and pleading in behalf of perishing souls in the Foreign Missions. He often, during this interval, made his confession and received Holy Communion; and it was on these occasions he gave the most tender proofs of having the College next his heart. It was when thus brought into closest union with his Blessed Lord in Holy Communion that the feeling of passing away for ever became strongest, and he prayed with great emotion that the Directors who had laboured with him, as well as the students, who were his glory and his joy, would not be left orphans. Now that the recovery of the patient was pronounced hopeless, Dr. Moriarty sent the sad news to Archbishop Murray. His Grace's reply is at once an affectionate message of condolence, and a conspicuous testimony of his attachment to one, whom he uniformly treated with a cordial, open, and generous assistance in carrying out a heavenly mission :—

"RAHAN LODGE, TULLAMORE,
"20th May, 1846.

"REV. DEAR SIR,
 "The intelligence contained in your letter of yesterday "was indeed inexpressib'y painful. The virtuous sufferer has "been employed by an All-bountiful Providence for the com- "mencement of a glorious work. Let us hope that the Divine "Architect will watch over the consummation of it, and that if "He be about to call this indefatigable labourer to the reward of "his toils, He will vouchsafe to raise up a substitute, filled with "his spirit, to take his place. . . . . You may commu- "nicate to him my blessing, and the assurance that, whether "his passage out of this scene of trouble be near or distant, my "humble, but earnest prayers for him shall not be wanting.

"I have the honor to remain,
 "Rev. dear Sir,
  "Very faithfully yours,
   "† D. MURRAY.
"Rev. D. MORIARTY."

Father Hand was thus spending his last days in pious reflections, asking forgiveness of all his sins, and in fervent petitions to God for those who were to succeed to his work, until he went to heaven, in the thirty-ninth year of his age and the eleventh of his Sacred Ministry, on Ascension Eve, 20th May, 1846, after having presided over All

Hallows for nearly four years. Some time before eight o'clock on the evening of that day, when the cold hand of Death began to fall upon him, he sent for the eight Directors, then associated with him, to hear his last injunction. For over ten minutes he spoke to them feelingly of their sacred duty of training good Missionaries for the famishing souls abroad, and then having recommended Dr. Moriarty as his successor, to preside over the College, his voice declined into the gentlest whisper, in which he could be heard saying over and over again, " Love one another." It was a scene which must have gladdened the angels, to behold him raise his feeble hand, supported by one of his colleagues, and hear him pronouncing upon the others, who had fallen upon their knees, his last blessing. Then he bade them farewell for ever, adding:—" You have done for me all " that was possible ; I am very happy. I have " had all I could desire, and I am now going " before my God with well-grounded confidence." After this there was a pause for a moment, when this great servant of God, with faint utterance, asked Dr. Woodlock, who was bending over him, for the last absolution. No more words were heard from him, but his lips could be seen moving in response to the prayers for a soul departing, which were recited aloud by those still kneeling; and as his head sank upon the pillow he kissed the crucifix, which his hand grasped until it was made rigid in death. At this supreme moment the bulk of the students were with Dr. Moriarty before the Altar in the College Chapel, beseeching God that their holy founder might himself be admitted into heaven, which he opened to so many. It was truly a holy death this of Father Hand, and of it may be repeated with peculiar fitness what St. Bernard said of the death of our countryman, St. Malachy:—" Precious is the life " of the saints; abundantly precious is the end of " their labours—the consummation of victory, the " gate of life, the ingress to perfect security."

On Saturday the 23rd of May, 1846, the remains were committed to the grave, and it was deeply affecting to see sobbing around the coffin, all the Students and Directors. The poor children of the neighbourhood, to whose religious instruction Father Hand had so sedulously devoted himself, wept also in their young sympathy, thus showing that his warm charity had shed its influence upon them. It was sad, very sad for these helpless children, and still more sorrowful for the orphaned students, and their afflicted staff, to gaze upon what had been to them the tokens of a father's care and a father's love, now changed into trappings of woe. It was mournful to think that the kind spirit, whom they always saw keeping watch had fled. He had been so much among them with his sweet disposition and cheerful greeting that they came to think he should be here for ever. Where is he now with his cordial welcome and kind word? That familiar figure they knew so well is covered with "six feet deep of clay," in the little cemetery, under the shadow of a ruin in the grounds of the College. It was, indeed, a message from Heaven that directed him to be laid in that ground now made holy by his relics. No mortuary chapel covers this sacred spot, and no sweet-smelling flowers perfume the air around it. His bones are not enshrined in gold and precious stones, but in crumbling walls, swathed in waving badges of that poverty which is the inheritance of his foundation.

The Students who are preparing for their distant Missions, and the Directors, whose duty is to teach them the Apostolic spirit as well as the Apostolic learning, go often to this simple grave of Father Hand, to meditate upon what he so constantly and practically taught. Kneeling there they cannot fail to be reminded forcibly of the devotedness of their holy founder, and encouraged to imitate his great virtues. And, when they raise their eyes from that grave to the simple wooden cross, which marks it, let them take consolation from the fact that through the merits of the cross Father Hand is enjoying his reward in heaven; for while the Holy Ghost has said :—" Weep for "the dead for his light hath failed," the same Holy Spirit added:—"Weep but a little, for he is at rest." He is surely at rest, and may he rest in peace!

Indeed, no higher tribute, under Heaven, can be paid to the memory of Father Hand, than to come into the presence of his Foreign Missionary College, which crowns this northern suburb of Dublin, and pour out one's soul by that precious earth which covers his resting place. And, the offer of this tribute always gives happiness in All Hallows. There is great joy when its Missionaries from time to time, after many wanderings in the hot plains of India, Australia, or over the rough seas and prairies of other foreign lands, arrive "heavy laden with the spoil of harvests "rich" to visit at the humble shrine of their spiritual father. But, the hearts of Students and Directors dilate as they run to welcome some veteran soldiers of the cross, with heads white from years, and bodies spent with toil, coming to pray around the grave of Father Hand. The veneration all these retain for him will speak our gratitude, and will also claim their indulgence for the many shortcomings of this feeble effort to tell the story of his meritorious career.

The character of Father Hand brings up the deep and earnest love of God, which coming to him in his youth hot, so to speak, from the purifying furnace of adversity, permeates every action of his life. One cannot recall without emotion the pinching circumstances, the humiliations in which he received his early training for the ministry. His exemplary meekness, his simplicity, a most austere, but unassuming piety, with many other virtues that could be named, find a high place in his history. Indeed it were meet to tarry a moment here in the consideration of these many special features of the man, but among them there are two more marked than the rest. These were a stern devotion to what he believed to be the call of God, and an abiding spirit of labour. It is necessary to retrace the life of Father Hand to appreciate rightly his unconquerable determination. He did not get credit for intellectual vigour, owing to his nature, in which there was not a particle of ostentation, but every one awarded him a great moral force. It has been told how, while yet young, he resolved to obey his vocation to the priesthood, and kept his resolution despite his father's opposition and slender means. Day after day, as has already been stated, for four years he had to walk eight miles, sometimes in rain and snow for the education needed to enter Maynooth, and after being admitted, it became an imperatve necessity with him, in order to defray the expenes of his College, to combine weighty office duties with an arduous course of studies It is not too much to say that the example of Father Hand's fortitude in these difficulties has strewn flowers where many a pious youth sees but thorns.

This phase of Father Hand's force of will does not, however, compare with the triumph he achieved by his inflexible devotedness to the cause of the Foreign Missions. Believing he had a call from God to dedicate himself to this object, upon it he fastened with characteristic resolution, and acted accordingly throughout his life, with a tenacity absolutely invincible. Many a solemn warning he received not to engage in this undertaking, since it was beyond his strength. Discouragements, as we have amply shown, fell upon him thick and fast, but they melted before his indomitable determination. If opposition threatened he pressed on with unremitting energy, gathering his forces as he advanced until the danger disappeared. How effectively he was helped by a confidence in God is well-known to those who enjoyed his acquaintance. It was well kown that, because of this reliance on the Divine assistance, no adverse influence could thwart his design. He even made a public profession of his faith in this respect, by invariably meeting the reasons urged against him, with the answer:—"God is good; "God is good." This was haply brought out on one occasion at a meeting of the leading clergy, summoned by Archbishop Murray, to deliberate on the immediate opening of the Catholic College for the Foreign Missions. Among those present there happened to be one, who from the beginning was most pronounced in his distrust of Father Hand's ability to execute an enterprise of such magnitude. He was occupying the time of the meeting almost exclusively by urging against Father Hand arguments, based on what were alleged to be insurmountable obstacles, while the only reply that came from the object of attack was :—"God is good ; God is good." At last Dr. Murray interposed to this effect :—" Yes, Father " Hand, God is good to those like you, who have "the courage and devotion to accomplish His " Divine will fearlessly." These words, uttered incisively from the chair, silenced the enemy, but it is right to add that he who showed this hostility, waited upon Father Hand a few years afterwards with ample apology and reparation.

It was this firm dependence on God that constituted Father Hand's triumphant resistance to opposition in the great work he set himself to do —it made him powerful in his power, wise by his wisdom, and happy by his happiness. By this, and a genuine simplicity, an unselfish zeal, he won the respect and love of many friends. In the familiarity of domestic intercourse his kindness was a well-spring never exhausted, but always running over. This grace of kindness—for it is a grace, and a great grace—bore fruit even outside the household of faith. His mission of charity brought him often in contact with the highest in the land. It was natural, especially in his time, that they who had been accustomed to trample on poor Catholics, should be disposed to treat with contempt the ministers of the hated religion. Nevertheless, he was proud to be known as a Catholic priest. His tone was confident and manly, like that of St. Paul before Festus, but thére breathed all the while in what he said and did that spirit of mildness which was able to dissipate prejudice; so that by-and-by his simple candour, his kind-hearted geniality, gained him the favour of every one who had to do with him. And this esteem was not confined to those who knew him; it extended to those who had heard of his character, but had no personal knowledge of himself. And why not? for there is no one who must not admire the example of a man like Father Hand, struggling and struggling successfully to do holy work.

The second characteristic which distinguished Father Hand's life was his spirit of labour. And how abundant in good works was that short life? In considering his career, one sees him as we have already depicted, in the morning of his days, a little boy walking with his mother to the parish chapel for his first communion, and thus establish that intimate union with his divine Lord, which he ever after maintained. Then the earnest heroism of his mid-day, and the golden glories of his even-tide! How beautiful are these achievements of good work! They are more resplendent than the most polished marble, and more lasting than brass. Surely here in this College words are not needed to describe them. They are written on these spacious grounds, on the very leaves of these grand old trees, even the very walls of the buildings show in their outward look, the spirit of labour he possessed in such eminent degree. True, Dr. Moriarty, Dr. Woodlock, Dr. Bennett and others had a large share in these marvellous results; but it was Father Hand who originated the movement, breathed life and form into it, and possessed the broad mind, and brave heart to defy the storm that threatened its infancy. In telling his story, therefore, there is no desire to diminish the glory which is due to the devoted and able men, associated with him, and who were faithfully at his side, cheering him in his difficulties. Their glory will not be dimmed by his praise; for it is no disparagement to brave officers to be led by a great captain. " I have planted," said the apostle, " Apollo watered, but God gave the increase ": . . . Now he that planteth, and he " that watereth are one. And every man shall " receive his own reward according to his own "labour."* And great, indeed, is the merit of these zealous colleagues of Father Hand. "Their "reward is with the Lord, and the care of them "with the Most High. Therefore shall they "receive a kingdom of glory, and a crown of beauty " at the hand of the Lord." †

Father Hand appeared when the old faith of his fathers was just reviving from passive forbearance, to an assertion of its rights, and he was one of its best champions. By his indefatigable zeal in the propagation of this old faith he imparted vigour to its purpose, and it now bears the impression of his activity. He went about in its cause as if the words of the Apostle were ever ringing in his ears :—" Be thou vigilant, labour in "all things, do the work of an Evangelist, fulfil thy "ministry." Thus did the great servant of God work with the vigour and energy of a strong man till it pleased his Divine Master to bid him enter into his eternal rest. It is a melancholy reflection that a career so full of usefulness to mankind and glory to God should have been thus early arrested. He had laboured only for eleven years in the ministry, but he was always up during this brief span as soon as the " gray streaks " began to appear on the sky, and worked till long after sundown. How rich in results these eleven years, how numerous the trophies of this

* I. Ep. to the Corinth. iii. 6, 7, 8. † Wisdom v. 16, 17.

short campaign, has been now told imperfectly but affectionately.

The strong and ardent labourer is dead, and the plough is overturned in the furrow; for his work ceased in the spring-time. He has however, sown enough for those who come after him to reap an abundant harvest. He has laid deep foundations for others to build a lasting monument. Those who have succeeded to his work pray that they may be made worthy of the trust bequeathed to them by such a man, and they have no fear that God will make his Foreign Missionary College flourish in the future as He has done in the past. Forty-two years ago it began with one student, and the present year has numbered 1,741 as having passed, since its foundation, through its halls. Of these students 1,192 became priests, and have gone forth to do the work of the ministry in all parts of the earth. Now, if one considers what even a few zealous missionaries can do, he is amazed at the extraordinary fruitfulness with which God has blessed the work begun by Father Hand. Nearly 1,200 priests from a College that opened with but one student forty-two years ago! And all this without any aid almost, save that of poor Ireland! Surely God will continue to bless Father Hand's foundation, and enable it to carry out still more successfully his high and holy object. This is the humble but firm confidence of those to whom Father Hand has bequeathed his mission, and their prayer constantly is that they may water well what he has planted, so that God may give the increase.

CHAPTER XIII.

A PORTRAIT.

> CONTENTS.—Father Hand lived the life of ardent faith, and died the death of the Saints—He sacrificed his life in the pursuit of a high and glorious purpose—He had the stone over the great door of All Hallows inscribed with the words, "Going therefore, teach ye all nations"—The paramount concern to which all are bound is to save their souls—The Sacraments are the means by which this can be effected—Father Hand dedicated himself to the bringing of these means within the reach of the spiritually-destitute—That God should make salvation depend on conformity with these external rites is not without explanation—God appointed *priests* to be "the dispensors of these mysteries," and Father Hand dedicated himself to the education of young priests—The admirable portrait of the great St. Columba or Columbkille—The features of Father Hand traced in this portrait—The curriculum of studies that has come down from Father Hand in All Hallows—The gratitude due to all those who have taken part in Father Hand's blessed work—To make All Hallows worthy of the memory of Father Hand is to complete the risen glory of the Irish Church.

IN the circumstances of Father Hand's departure from this world, for which he had done so much, to the Throne of God, whose honour and glory he had successfully advanced, we had the happiness of seeing what is the death of the Saints. He lived the life of ardent faith, and he died the death of a martyr. Had his health been better cared, he would have remained longer here below, to edify the world by his devotion in the pursuit of a high and glorious purpose. He was sent by his Divine Master to helpless sinners of the present time, as the Hebrew fishermen were deputed to the Gentiles of old, for his mission was a faithful counterpart to theirs in the successful application of persons and resources immeasurably inadequate to the task. It was, perhaps, this striking resemblance that caused him to have the massive granite over the great door of the old Manor-house at All Hallows inscribed with the words:— "Going therefore, teach ye all nations." Thus, he had always before his eyes the commission which Jesus gave to His Apostles. He kept the words of this solemn charge also in his heart, and we know how passionately he gave them expression in devoting himself to the relief of starving souls. And, indeed, he could not have sacrificed his life in a higher or holier cause than in bringing within the reach of the spiritually-destitute the means of saving their souls—the only work properly so called—"the one thing necessary" for all men to accomplish.

Every one in this world—high and low, rich and poor—has obligations according to his position in life. The man of business must be active, the farmer must be industrious, to succeed. There are duties peculiar to the good mother as to the father, and again as to the children. But there is one paramount concern to which all are bound alike, and this is to save their souls. Each one has got a soul, and God will require it of him. There is a man born to riches, and to all the pleasures that follow in their train; but what are they all worth if he save not his soul? The parents work hard to increase their substance, and so gain an independence for their family—a very good work to be sure, and a necessary one; yet it is all nothing, and infinitely worse than nothing, if they purchase it at the cost of their souls. There is the young daughter, beneficent and fair, so that the people bid blessings on her head as she passes by; this is of no account if she lose her immortal soul. And there is the poor man suffering hunger and privations of various kinds; surely the lot of such a one is miserable indeed if he suffer, in addition, the loss of his soul.

Now, the Sacraments are the means left by God in His Church, by which the soul can be saved, and it was in the effort of making these means available to all who are in need that Father Hand began to draw too liberally on his limited strength in the very first stages of his mission at Phibsboro'. He was so busy there, and so exhausted by his labours that one would think he could not take up anything else, and yet he gave time and energy to more severe work outside his own proper field. In our city hospitals, especially those under Protestant management, there was, in Father Hand's time, more, perhaps, than there is now, an abundant scope for the zeal of a holy priest. A patient lying on his sick bed, suddenly trembles as some horrible sensation creeps over him. Presently he is on the ground shrieking with pain, and gathered into a knot by the writhings of a fearful agony. In a few minutes the racking torture has broken the frame. The limbs collapse and the soul goes to its last account. How happily that poor Catholic patient would have died, if a priest had been there to shrive him! Father Hand's activity in being on the spot for such cases was something wonderful. Every Sunday, as soon as he could steal away from his other duties, and on many week days, he flew silently and swiftly to those places where he believed the Destroyer was committing greatest havoc. He was abroad at midnight as well as in the day-time, and when the storm swept past, and the sun came out again, the tongues which spoke eternal gratitude to Father Hand had multiplied exceedingly. Then from the hospital he frequently went, under official permission, to the prison and the penitentiary, to console the wretched and despairing, or soften the hardened criminal.

It happened at this time that a clerical friend from the country called at Phibsboro' on Sunday, to visit Father Hand, and, as a matter of course, failed to find him in the house. "Would Father "Hand be back in the evening?" he asked. "Not until it is late," was the answer of the servant, who added with emphasis, "*And God* "*knows how late it may be.*" The visitor, as he turned away from the door, met Dean Dowley, and after a cordial greeting, mentioned his disappointment.

The Dean smiled and then spoke to the following effect:—" My dear friend, is it to find Father "Hand here on a Sunday? Enumerate the "dungeons in the city where criminals under "sentence of death await their doom, and those "in which the reprobate hatches the repetition "of his crime. Go there, or into any of the "asylums for the unfortunate, and you will "be sure to find him in some of these places; "but not here. He has got general powers "from the Bishop, and he is using them more "like a martyr than an Apostle."

But, is it not strange, not to say altogether improbable, that God should make salvation depend on conformity with certain simple external forms? It is not for us to investigate the inscrutable ways of Divine Providence. Whatever be the reason, it is beyond doubt that God has instituted certain rites in His Church which are visible signs of invisible grace—that is Sacraments; and of these, Baptism is the first and necessary, not only as a condition, but as a means of salvation. The reason why it is so is hidden, like many other things, from us; but the fact is as certain as that God is truth essentially. And yet this truth is not, after all, without explanation.

Everywhere in the world around us there are indications of a marvellous intelligence and wisdom—indications which, when considered attentively, force upon any thoughtful man the conviction that the Author of this world is infinite intelligence. The reflection is commonplace, if, indeed, so sublime a reflection ever can be commonplace. But let one stand on the sea-shore, and look out over the vast expanse that stretches away beyond the distant horizon into boundless space; let one gaze into the blue vault overhead on a bright night, and try to reckon the stars, or trace their courses, or penetrate the illimitable depths beyond, till the imagination is overpowered. Again, let one pause to think amidst the solitude or majesty of mountain scenery in the quiet pensiveness of evening, and if he be capable of rising from effect to cause, he must recognize a Being infinitely wise in this work. And the more science and observation extend our acquaintance with the universe, whether in its vastness on the one hand, or in the examination of every part of it in detail, the more do we discover the Divine character of the power that created it. The same infinite intelligence is discovered in the minutest part—a point invisible to the naked eye—as in those larger features, which astound the imagination by their immensity.

These reflections are trite; but it is, nevertheless, useful to recall them, because many who are lost in admiration of the wisdom displayed in the stupendous mechanism of the earth, will not recognize anything supernatural in the kingdom which God came on earth to establish. As His kingdom is not of this world, people who will not look beyond the fashion of this world fail to see any fitness in the things of the Church. There is a darkness that comes from the heart, and it is no wonder that they, who love this darkness more than the light, cannot see. The Divine beauty of the Church of Christ is recognized with reverence by her children, and even those who entertained for her no other than feelings of the deepest hate, have, amidst the looks of fierce jealousy with which they followed her, been forced to exclaim:— "How beautiful are thy tents, O Israel!" The Redeemer founded His Church for man, and described it, therefore, as a city upon a mountain; a sheep-fold, a kingdom on earth, though not the earth, to which obedience was made a duty.

His Church is, therefore, a visible body, distinguished by signs of its own; and so the Sacraments, through which God, by a heavenly dispensation, maintains the inner life of the faithful, are at the same time the external badges of the Christian profession. Hence, on the grounds of common sense, we must recognize the eternal fitness of things in these sensible signs of invisible grace, which exist in the Kingdom of Christ here below.

By Baptism we are made members of the mystic body of Christ, thus becoming His adopted brethren, and co-heirs to His kingdom; and we have the Sacrament of Confirmation to strengthen us in the conflict with the enemies of our Faith from within and without. Then, as the days pass, and perchance we fall into sin, there is the Sacrament of Penance to raise us up again and again One of the best gifts man has received from God is free will, and this was bestowed upon him in order that by it he may be ever acting in a manner pleasing to God. But man often turns this free will against God, by breaking the Divine Commandments, and this is sin. Hence, the power of forgiving sin is the highest that God Himself can exercise; and it is one of His greatest mercies to have appointed in the Church a body of men who shall exercise this Divine power in His place. In one of those sublime conferences which the Redeemer had with the Apostles during the interval between Easter and the Ascension, He said to them:—" Whose sins you shall forgive, they are forgiven them," not they *shall* be forgiven, but *are* forgiven by your very act. Of course, this power which God conferred on the Apostles for sake of the Church, He gave for sake of that Church, so long as it should endure in the world, and in this way the Divine power of forgiving sins, which He gave to the first priests, has been handed on by them to their successors. Thus we have in the Church of Christ a great charter of Divine love, which has passed down from the Apostles to the priesthood of our own day.

After Penance, there is the most adorable Sacrament of the Eucharist to renew our strength, and make us young like the eagle. And when the time comes round for each one to make choice of a state of life, God has instituted in His Church the Holy Sacrament of Matrimony, to bless the bridegroom and the bride; and the Sacrament of Holy Orders for him who undertakes the responsibilities of the Ministry. And, last of all, when Death comes, there is the sweet and touching Sacrament of Extreme Unction, to comfort the dying, and carry the hopes of the trembling soul heavenward.

To secure the administration of these saving Sacraments for the great many, who would otherwise be left to die without them, was the grand aim which Father Hand proposed to himself. God appointed *priests* to be "the dispensers of these mysteries," and Father Hand dedicated his life to the education of young *priests* for the Foreign Missions, especially wherever the Irish emigrant had settled. There is no more striking token of our Saviour's love for us than the institution of this priesthood—that glorious company, who appeared so radiant with virgin beauty in the Vision of the New Jerusalem, seen by the Apostle St. John, and described by him in the Apocalypse. This is that Ecclesiastical Hierarchy which has ever been the object of deepest veneration to the faithful children of Christ, and of the fiercest persecution to His enemies. One cannot eulogize too highly a dignity borne by Jesus himself, who was priest and prophet. And, of a truth, a priest cannot fairly be charged with self-praise if he speak of the exalted prerogatives of his sacred office, for his title to this nobility is, that he is the "dispenser of the mysteries of God." And yet the number of those in the world who have no share in these beneficent dispensations, is so great as to be quite appalling. There are millions upon millions of human beings who have never been baptized who have never heard the truths of salvation, who have never seen a priest. This is why, in the silence of midnight at All Hallows, the heart of

Father Hand was wrung with the same grief as that of our great St. Columba or Columbkille in the solitude of Iona. It was for this reason that Father Hand in All Hallows, like his prototype in Iona, consecrated himself to the Divine mission of saving souls.

Adamnan, the biographer of St. Columba, says of him:—"Angelic in appearance, eloquent in "address, holy in work, with talents of the highest "order and consummate prudence, he lived a "good soldier of Christ during thirty-five years "in his adopted island (Iona). He never could "spend the space of even one hour without study "or prayer, or writing, or some other holy occu-"pation; and so incessantly was he engaged night "and day in the unwearied exercise of watching "and of corporal austerities, that the weight of "his singular labour would seem beyond the power "of human endurance; and still he was beloved by "all, for a holy joy, ever beaming in his face, "revealed the ecstacies with which the Holy "Spirit filled his inmost soul." In this admirable portrait consists whatever now remains to be written of Father Hand.

Adamnan tells us that "St. Columba, in the "forty-second year of his age (563), resolving to "seek a foreign country for the love of Christ, "sailed from Ireland to Britain," as Scotland was then called. He was graciously welcomed by

s

Conall King of the Albanian Scots, and a relative of his own, who gave him the island of Hy or Iona. St. Columba had twelve disciples with him, and laid the foundation of the Monastery of Hy. which soon became the most famous in Northern Europe, and for centuries after the recognized head of his order. From Iona he ventured to carry the light of Christianity among the heathen, and, with God's blessing, he planted the standard of the Cross in the Orkney Isles, in the Hebrides, among the Northern Picts, and away South beyond the mountains, over the Lowlands, and into Northumbria. Amidst all these labours he found time for the cultivation of letters; and his literary productions are a title, second only to his imperishable services in the cause of God, to the gratitude and veneration of mankind. He is said to have built three hundred abbeys, and to have written as many manuscript books, some of which have survived to the present day. He thus practised what he prescribed by rule, namely, that sanctity and learning should go together in the training of his disciples. By this plan, through the blessing of God, he was able to send forth missionaries, who not merely cultivated the devastated plains, but bore a chief part in the reconstruction of a new civilzation in Europe.

So, too, Father Hand, on a wooded slope, beautifully situated a little to the North of Dublin, founded a Foreign Missionary College, where the students are exercised in sanctity and science. His life was too short, and his hands were too full in collecting funds for the support of his institution, to be able to write books; but, in the midst of his overwhelming cares, he gave many hours at a time to teaching poor children. Thus, by his own example, he impressed upon the students of All Hallows the important lesson that, in their pressing labours on the Foreign Missions, they ought to make the education of the young a special object of their care. And an obstinate fight they have to sustain in the faithful discharge of this trust, confided to them by their Spiritual Father. In most of their Missions they find the schools under the control of a very powerful and influential party, who boldly declare that children ought to be taught the branches of secular knowledge without the active presence of religion while this knowledge is being imparted. That in the colonies particularly, where the population is *mixed*, it is necessary to have the youth of all religions taught together in the same school, where no mention whatever of religion is to be made by the teachers while giving instruction. Let the pupils go afterwards to their priests or respective clergymen, and learn religion from them if they choose. But Father Hand's Missionaries, true to the spirit of their founder, maintain that religion ought to be present and actively engaged—that religion and knowledge ought not to be separated, for on their union in the schools depends the formation of the character of the children.

Again, the name of St. Columba is too great to be confined to Ireland, or to any particular district of Ireland; it is the possession of the whole nation, and belongs by very dear ties to Caledonia and North Britain. He is, however, the family property of the races in old Tyrconnell, where, sprung from a Royal line, both through his father and mother, he threw away his claim to the Sovereignty of Ireland, which he might expect by descent, and devoted himself to God's service, with that deep fervent piety, that enthusiastic zeal, that ardent attachment, which were his special characteristics. In the same way the fame of Father Hand's labours has been passing beyond the limits of his own country, until it reached the remotest spots where the English language is spoken. His College, since its foundation forty-two years ago, has sent Missionaries to England and Scotland, to the Canadas, to the East and West Indies, to the Cape of Good Hope, to Tasmania, and New Zealand, in the South Pacific; to America, North and South, and other places abroad, thus adding to the splendid army by which Ireland has, from the time of St. Columba, extended the Kingdom of Christ.

St. Columba passed from his fosterage in Tyrconnell to the School of St. Finian at the head of Stranford Lough, and made a course of studies under this famous master. Thence he went to Clonard and other celebrated schools, so that he became a great scholar as well as a great saint. In pointing out his literary labours before, the fact was mentioned that St. Columba made learning second only to sanctity not alone in his own education but in that of his disciples, and it was precisely in this that Father Hand shows the most striking resemblance to the founder of Iona.

We saw that Father Hand's first care in entering upon his great enterprise was to surround himself not only with holy but *able* colleagues; and by an express clause in his rule, the student who did not give proof of satisfactory progress in his studies was obliged to leave. Then he required every candidate for admission to pass such an examination in the Latin and Greek Classics, and Elementary Mathematics as would enable him to begin Philosophy. This was in order to put the mind through a preliminary discipline, so that after a certain time the young man can bring to his professional studies reasoning powers highly cultivated, for there is no better means for this than Philosophy.

The human mind does not rest content with knowing simply that such a fact is or has been.

It always seeks to know why it is, or how comes it to be so. This second kind of knowledge is variously called Philosophical, Scientific or Rational knowledge, to distinguish it from Historical and Empirical knowledge, which is sometimes called the knowledge of fact. Science, therefore, and Philosophy, in the widest acceptation of these terms, mean the same thing. Science or Scientific knowledge is broadly understood to be the knowledge of the reasons of things, or the knowledge of the causes on which things depend. Now, in this interesting process of seeking the reasons of the things or events that come under our apprehension, we view these things as effects, and at once look for the causes to which to refer them, and these causes we view also as effects of higher causes. Thus we proceed to ascend through the series of effects and causes, until we arrive at the highest causes to which our faculties can attain.

As an illustration one enters a mill moved by water-power. He sees there quite a number of effects, all which refer at once to the action of various parts of machinery as the immediate cause. But then he inquires what is the cause of the motion of the machinery, and he finds it is moved by the great wheel, and the great wheel is moved by water. Nor does he stop here. He inquires what is the reason of this effect produced by the water? On the exterior face of the rim of the wheel are projections at fixed intervals. The water is brought to fall on one side of the wheel, and the downward motion of the wheel on one side brings fresh projections from above under the water, which falling in a continuous column, gives a continuous motion to the wheel. Thus, the effects produced in the mill are traced to the weight of falling water, or in other words, to the general law of gravitation. In the same way we trace the movement of the hands on the dial of an ordinary clock through a series of effects and causes up to the same law of gravitation, and the law of gravitation itself may be viewed as an effect of some higher cause. And a thousand other phenomena may be traced to the same great law of gravitation.

From this study of things in the concrete or in detail the mind rises to the study of their general laws or principles, and this knowledge is called philosophy or the science of the ultimate reasons of things, and the body of sciences, called philosophy, is a collection of the sciences which inquire into the ultimate reasons of things, not the absolutely ultimate, but the highest reason which we can attain.

The division of the philosophical sciences may be various according to the principle on which it is based. Looking to the object matter of philosophical science, the highest generalization of things that can be made the object of thought is *Being* in general, and the part of philosophy which treats of this is called *Ontology*. Then passing from the consideration of *Being* in general to that of beings as they exist in fact, the Creator, the great Being who stands at the head of all other beings—God—comes first for consideration. The part of philosophy which treats of the Creator or God, is called *Theodicy*. Passing from the Creator we come at once to the consideration of the created Universe, and the part of philosophy that treats of this vast aggregate of corporeal beings, their general laws and facts, that is the Cosmos, is called *Cosmology*. Under this head are contained the important science of Physics and Mathematics. Then comes the inquiry into the laws and constitution of animate beings, and among animate beings, the study of man himself is, of course, one of paramount importance. The science which treats of the constitution or faculties of the human mind, is called *Psychology*, and is often set down as Philosophy *par excellence*. But as man is specially distinguished by his intellectual faculty, his power of apprehending, judging and reasoning, it is manifestly proper to treat specially of the exercise of this great faculty, and the science occupied with this matter is called *Logic*. Lastly, man is not only an intellectual being, he is also a moral being, bound to conform his actions to a moral law, and the science which treats of him as a moral being is called *Moral Philosophy*.

Now it is hardly possible to overrate the healthy development which will accrue to the faculties of the mind from the exercise of this study. Milton expressed this beautifully when he wrote :—

> " How charming is divine Philosophy !
> Not harsh and rugged as dull fools suppose,
> But musical as is Apollo's lute,
> And a perpetual feast of nectared sweets,
> Where no crude surfeit reigns."

Hence there is in All Hallows a graduated course of Philosophy extending over two years, and divided into Logic, Metaphysics, Psychology, and Moral Philosophy or Ethics. In the treatment of the Philosophical Sciences it is obviously convenient to begin with Logic, because it is the object of Logic to cultivate the intellectual faculty, which we use in all the sciences. Its proper office is to furnish such aids to the intellect as scientific culture can towards forming correct perceptions, judgments and reasonings, and, therefore, an acquaintance with it is so useful, if not necessary, in the prosecution of high ecclesiastical studies that Father Hand imposed it as a condition for admission into his College that, "*the candidate shall pass an " Examination for the Logic Class.*"

Again, considering the Philosophical Sciences from the point of view of method, the object matter of Philosophy is divided into two parts, the one called the rational, the other the Experimental and Mathematical. Hence it has come down in All Hallows to make the study of the Experimental and Mathematical Sciences co-ordinate with the course of rational Philosophy, during the first two years, and at the same time to teach the students English Literature with some of the modern languages.

When the mind has thus been trained to think and to reason well, it is able to take up an exact course of instruction in Scripture, Theology, Canon Law, Ecclesiastical History, preaching and the other duties of the pastoral office, with ease and success. In these professional studies the plan, inherited from Father Hand, is directed to make the student's stock of knowledge clear and definite, and accordingly the programme in All Hallows is more concerned as to the *quality* than the *quantity*. And, indeed, the greatest evil of our time is that men try to know too much, and it is the direction which the spirit of this age takes. The effort is to know a great many things, to appear not to be inferior to any other man, and the necessary consequence is that nothing is known well.

In these special studies it is, no doubt, of the highest importance to propose questions, and to write down answers to them from one's own storehouse; but the slavish copying of another's remarks is doing what may be done mechanically by a copying press. So, too, the practice of disputation is useful, but open to its evils as well as to its advantages. It is good to acquire a freedom of speech, but it is also good to learn the art of listening. The fluent talker may be more brilliant, and it is often mortifying to have one's arguments not heard, while the arguments of the other side are sounded by a fluent and bold adversary. But taking it all in all, it may be questioned whether the better opportunities of exercising a calm judgment, of comparing reasons, and considering their force and relevancy may not more than compensate for the talking triumphs of the other. This, of course, is to be understood when Ecclesiastical Students in prosecuting their professional studies argue for truth, for in their discussions particularly, if the water be disturbed by noisy or angry repartee, one cannot see to the bottom.

Then the influence of St. Columba exercises a marvellous power amongst us to this day. He can still be traced all over the land—on the hills and in the villages, in the recesses of the mountains, and by the shores of the melancholy ocean. Though the monuments of his heroic zeal be now sparse and almost effaced, we can easily discern them, still living in the traditions of the people. Similarly the blessed work of Father Hand has left its mark on the length and breadth of this Island. Even in its remotest glens and villages there is hardly one who has not experienced some proof of his zeal.

There are very few, if any, in this country, who have not either a friend or relative, perhaps a son or a daughter, a sister or a brother in some remote quarter of the globe, and these, without doubt, came under the influence of Father Hand's missionaries, who took care not only of their eternal interests, but elevated their social position by teaching them self-respect.

It was a glorious season that when Ireland was covered with the works of St. Columba. The pious and learned of every age speak of it, and they express their joyous feelings in the elevated imagery of the inspired writings. And, indeed, it is only inspired language that can depict the first growth of the Christian seed in Erin. In the prophetic words of Isaias:—" The land that was "desolate and impassable, shall be glad, and the "wilderness shall rejoice, and shall flourish like the "lily. It shall bud forth and blossom, and shall "rejoice with joy and praise." Thus did the garden of the early Irish Church yield the saving fruits of Christian faith in great abundance. The blessing of St. Columba remained on the Island, and the succession of the Irish priesthood was by a marvellous providence kept unbroken. The faith was handed on from father to son all through our evil days—a legacy rendered very dear to the people, which lightened the burthen of their woe, and strengthened their sickening hope. The winter—that dread winter—passed and a new spring dawned upon the land. One can look around and see what a change has been wrought even in a few generations. The human body of our Divine Lord lay dead and shut away out of sight in a cave for three days, and then rose again glorious and immortal. Even so the mystic body of Christ — the Church — in this country, barbarously crucified and transfixed, lay for dead, shut away out of sight in the caves and recesses of our mountains, for three days of centuries, and to-day, behold that body come forth from the tomb and once more living in the land. But, nowhere is this resurrection more striking or more glorious than in the work of Father Hand. His heroic apostles from Ireland are to be found abroad everywhere engaged in the laborious round of missionary work, while they are ever mindful of the noble effort to advance in Ecclesiastical perfection and learning.

"Perhaps, your lordship," wrote Father Hand, soon after the opening of All Hallows, in a few humble but touching words to some of the foreign Bishops, "can do something for the College "amongst the clergy and laity committed to your "pastoral care." And, now, in closing this history of his life and labours, it is truly pleasant to offer words of thankfulness to all those who have taken a part, and a substantial part, in his blessed work. " God wishes all men to be saved." The only responsible agents of this mercy must be those who can efficiently accomplish His designs. Father Hand's Missionary College gives activity to the Christian charity which desires to perform this great Catholic duty. The religious destitution of our Foreign and Colonial Missions has, through the voice, still living, of Father Hand, awakened the sympathy of the faithful in these kingdoms. Millions of Pagans subject to British rule, and multitudes of our own countrymen, scattered over the dependencies of the Empire, have hardly a hope, unless in the charity of those at home, who are bound to diffuse the blessings of salvation. It was to the missionary spirit, created by a conviction of this duty, our fathers were indebted for the light of the Gospel, and we are, ourselves, indebted for its hopes. The obligation can never be more urgent than, as in this case, when the preservation of the Faith among our brethren, and its propagation among our Pagan colonists are entirely dependent upon our Christian benevolence. The burden of the work has been already borne by our Irish Missionary College, without noise, calmly, gracefully, sweetly, joyously, just as the good husbandman rears the fruits and flowers that enrich and beautify his garden. Is it too much to expect now, that many will be found to count it a privilege —a proud privilege, which will be pointed to as an honour, to their descendants—to contribute to make All Hallows worthy of the memory of Father Hand, and the completion, so to speak, of the risen glory of the Irish Church?

www.ingramcontent.com/pod-product-compliance
Lightning Source LLC
Chambersburg PA
CBHW031326230426
43670CB00006B/257